Nicolas Malebranche

Nicolas Malebranche

His Philosophical Critics and Successors

Edited by Stuart Brown

1991

Van Gorcum, Assen/Maastricht, The Netherlands

© 1991 Van Gorcum & Comp. B.V., P.O.Box 43, 9400 AA Assen, The Netherlands

CIP-DATA KONINKLIJKE BIBLIOTHEEK, DEN HAAG

Nicolas

Nicolas Malebranche: his philosophical critics and successors/ed. by Stuart Brown. - Assen [etc.]: Van Gorcum
With index, ref.
Subject headings: philosophy/Malebranche, Nicolas.

ISBN 90 232 2570 8

Printed in The Netherlands by Van Gorcum, Assen

Contents

1   Introduction   4

                                              Stuart Brown

2   Bishop Pierre-Daniel Huet's Remarks on Malebranche   10

                                              Richard H Popkin

3   Foucher's Mistake and Malebranche's Break: Ideas,
     Intelligible Extension and the End of Ontology   22

                                              Richard A Watson

4   The Malebranche-Arnauld Debate: Philosophical or
     ideological?   35

                                              Harry Bracken

5   Divine and Human Will in the Philosophy of
     Malebranche   49

                                              Patrick Riley

6   Malebranche's Occasionalism and Leibniz's Pre-established
     Harmony: an 'Easy Crossing' or an Unbridgeable Gap?   81

                                              Stuart Brown

7   Malebranche and Locke: The Theory of Moral Choice, a
     Neglected Theme   94

                                              Jean Michel Vienne

8   Malebranche, Arnauld and Berkeley on the
     Imperceptibility of Outer Objects   109

                                              G.N.A. Vesey

9   Hume's Criticism of Malebranche's Theory of Causation: A
     Lesson in the Historiography of Philosophy   116

                                              John P. Wright

Bibliography   131
Index   161

                                                                  1

Acknowledgements

Versions of some of the papers that comprise this volume were presented in a draft form at a conference under the auspices of the British Society for the History of Philosophy, in November, 1987. The paper by Stuart Brown was also presented at the Leibniz Congress in 1988 and is due to appear in a Supplement to *Studia Leibnitiana.* That paper has been expanded for this volume. The remaining papers were commissioned for this volume. The paper by Patrick Riley is adapted from his book *The General Will before Rousseau,* with permission of the publishers, Princeton University Press.

The Editor is grateful to Dr. Niall Martin for translating the paper by Jean Michel Vienne. He would also like to acknowledge the help of Mrs Denise Powers, Philosophy Secretary at the Open University. It is due to her care and patience that the large project of keying in the volume and the seemingly endless corrections has been seen through. Laura Dimmock, New Technology Co-Ordinator for the Arts Faculty, has been a generous and resourceful support.

Abbreviation

The *Oeuvres Complètes de Malebranche*, ed. André Robinet (Paris: Vrin, 1958-67) are referred to throughout this volume by the abbreviation 'OCM' followed by the volume number and page number.

1   Introduction

STUART BROWN

Compared to contemporaries like Locke and Leibniz, Nicolas Malebranche (1638-1715) has been a relatively neglected philosopher. This is not true in his native France, where his works have been produced in a fine critical edition and where a high quality secondary literature is now available.[1] It has also become much less true of the English-speaking world, where Malebranche is receiving more attention than he has for three hundred years. The 1690s saw a flurry of translations of Malebranche's works into English and his philosophy, for a limited period, enjoyed a good deal of attention. The story of his reception in Britain has been told by Charles McCracken in an important study.[2] And there is an increasing recognition amongst teachers and students of philosophy in the English-speaking world that our understanding of late seventeenth and early eighteenth century philosophy is bound to be distorted if we do not take account of Malebranche. It has been argued[3], for instance, that the idea of a school of 'British empiricism' (including Locke,Berkeley and Hume) is a 'myth' based partly on a failure to give due weight to the important influence of Malebranche on Berkeley and Hume.

Malebranche's influence on these 'empiricists' is acknowledged in this volume by specially contributed chapters from Godfrey N.A. Vesey and John P. Wright.[4]   Malebranche's relation to Locke, however, has generally been supposed to be rather different. Locke was, in the first place, six years Malebranche's senior and so Malebranche is less likely to have been a formative influence on him in the way he could be on Berkeley and Hume. Locke was also the author of a highly critical 'Examination' of one of Malebranche's central doctrines.[5]   Nonetheless, as Jean Michel Vienne argues in

4

Chapter 7, Locke's view of Malebranche was by no means wholly negative.

Ever since the publication of Malebranche's *Recherche de la Vérité* in 1674-75, his work became the centre of controversy. Partly because it was an overtly Cartesian book in its loyalties it provoked a hostile reaction amongst the anti-Cartesians. One of these was the sceptic Simon Foucher (1644-96), about whom Richard A. Watson writes in Chapter 3. Another of the sceptics, Pierre-Daniel Huet (1630-1721)[6], made notes on the *Recherche* which Richard H. Popkin gives an account of in Chapter 2. Malebranche was not only criticised by philosophers but, more vehemently, by theologians. The Jesuit Louis Le Valois' attack, for instance, was particularly directed against the Cartesian view that extension was the essence of matter, a view that was widely taken to be subversive of the Catholic doctrine of transubstantiation.[7]

If the *Recherche* was Malebranche's most substantial work, an even greater controversy attached to the publication of his *Traité de la Nature et de la Grâce* in 1680. It was this work that turned a former admirer, Antoine Arnauld (1612-1694), into one of Malebranche's most persistent and bitter critics. Their controversy about the nature of ideas lasted for more than a decade. Harry Bracken, in Chapter 4, offers an account of why the controversy was so persistent.

As Bracken points out, the context of the Malebranche-Arnauld dispute is a theological one. A central part of the controversy between them concerns the nature of God's will – a topic that forms the main part of Patrick Riley's contribution in Chapter 5. On this matter Malebranche took a very different view from Descartes. According to Descartes, God's will is above any law and the so-called 'eternal truths' are themselves subject to it.[8] God could make the 'laws' of mathematics different from what they are, were He to so choose. According to Descartes' view, therefore, the world is good just because it is God who made it. It is not the way it is because it is good by some eternal standard of goodness that is independent of God's will. According to Malebranche, on the other hand, God's perfection is shown by the simplicity and orderliness of His decrees. There are not only laws of nature which are expressions of God's 'general will'. There are also 'laws of grace'. This emphasis on the orderliness of God's ways was at variance, as Riley points out, with the view of God's providence accepted by his critics. The *Traité* was put on the Index in 1690.

Embattled though he was, Malebranche continued to retain a number of followers and defenders. Amongst these the most significant was Leibniz. The relations between Leibniz and Malebranche have been explored in an important study by André Robinet. Although a critic on some matters (see, for instance, Chapter 6), Leibniz took an exceptional interest in Malebranche's philosophy, happily adopted some of his most controversial notions, attempted to imitate his style of writing and undertook defenses of him against some of his critics.[9]

One of the features of Malebranche's philosophy which made it attractive to some but objectionable to others was its tendency to idealism. Foucher thought that Leibniz's philosophy, like Malebranche's, was open to the objection that it made bodies redundant.[10] The tendency of Malebranchist philosophy to a outright denial of material bodies may partially explain how Arthur Collier could have arrived at his idealist system independently of Berkeley.[11] Few were able to give credence to idealism. But, for a number of philosophers in France and Italy, including G.S. Gerdil (1718-1802) from Savoy, Malebranche's philosophy remained a bastion against materialism.[12]

Malebranche's place in the history of philosophy may partly rest on his importance for understanding other philosophers such as Leibniz, Berkeley and Hume. There were, of course, followers in England, such as John Norris, Thomas Taylor and Arthur Collier, not to mention Samuel Johnson in colonial America. But Malebranchism in England quickly petered out, probably because of the corrective influence of Locke. In Italy and France, however, Malebranchism continued to be represented not only through the eighteenth century (by Gerdil and Keranflech, for instance) but into the nineteenth century as well, affecting philosophers such as Rosmini and Maine de Biran.[13] Moreover, in France, Malebranche's thought was not simply a trace element in the philosophical culture. It exercised a pervasive influence in directions he himself would have not encouraged.

The reason for this lies in a tendency of Malebranche's philosophy in the direction of Deism. His doctrine of 'laws of grace' might be seen as an extension of the desire for rational intelligibility into the workings of Providence – an extension of the Cartesian aspiration for a rationally intelligible Nature beyond what Descartes himself would have countenanced. So regarded, Malebranche may be thought of as having Cartesianised Christianity – to the horror of the orthodox, such as Bossuet,[14] but to the satisfaction of those with a Deist tendency, like Voltaire, who wished to retain a general providence but reject particular wills, miracles and other features of official Christianity. Malebranche was thus able to influence *philosophes* who condemned the kind of system that would be involved in anything properly described as 'malebranchisme'.[15]

Another aspect, though strictly alternative, of the tendency of Malebranche's philosophy to Cartesianise providence and promote a kind of deism is its tendency to Spinozism. A number of his critics, such as Locke[16], saw what they took to be a tendency both to monism and to fatalism and remarked on the affinity to Spinoza. Even Malebranche's allies, including Leibniz[17], were worried about such

6

tendencies and one of them, J.J. Dortous de Mairan managed to elicit from Malebranche himself an account of why he rejected the charge of Spinozism.[18]

It is well known that what is supposed to have attracted Malebranche to Cartesianism in the first place was his reading of Descartes', treatise On Man, when it was published in 1664. As an Oratorian Malebranche had a special commitment to the teachings of St Augustine and he appears to have been inspired by the Augustinian dimension he perceived in Descartes' writings. He seems not to have been an ambitious man and disliked the publicity his books attracted. But, whether desired or not, Malebranche's writings achieved a 'success' in his lifetime that exceeded that of Leibniz, Berkeley and even Locke. Much of this 'success' might be attributed to his having, as it seemed, 'Christianized Descartes'. But if, in his own day, his appearing to have Cartesianised Christianity ensured he would be attacked and even harrassed by the orthodox, it is owing to this aspect, never prominent in England, that he continued to exert a posthumous influence on 'le siècle des lumières'.[19]

Notes

1. The Bibliography attached to this volume covers much of that literature so far as it relates to the theme of Malebranche's critics and successors up to the end of the eighteenth century. See the section on Bibliographies for other bibliographies of the Malebranche literature.

2. *Malebranche and British Philosophy* (Oxford: Clarendon Press, 1983).

3. See Norton (David Fate), "The myth of 'British Empiricism'", *History of European Ideas* 1 (1981) : 331-344.

4. Vesey's paper, as well as those by Watson, Brown and Vienne, was originally presented at a conference in London in November, 1987.

5. Locke's *An Examination of P. Malebranche's Opinion of Our Seeing All Things in God* was written in 1693 but only published posthumously in 1706. (See Bibliography.)

6. Huet was the author of *Censura philosophiae cartesianae*, (Paris, 1689). Leibniz sought unsuccessfully to have his own *Animadversiones in partem generalem Principiorum Cartesianorum* included in a later edition of Huet's book.

7.	The Congregation of the Index placed a limited ('donec corrigantur') condemnation on the errors of Descartes' metaphysics in 1663 which identified the problem posed for the Eucharist as orthodox Catholics understood it.

8.	Descartes makes his position very clear in the Sixth Set of Replies to Objections, Sect. 8, Adam & Tannery, *Oeuvres de Descartes* VII: 435-6, trans. Cottingham, Stoothoff and Murdoch, *The Philosophical Writings of Descartes* (Cambridge University Press, 1984) Vol. 2: 293f.

9.	For Leibniz's interest in Malebranche see Robinet (André), *Leibniz et Malebranche*. For an example of Leibniz's borrowing from Malebranche, see *Theodicy* 204-8. Leibniz also attempted Malebranche-style dialogues such as his 'Entretien de Philarete et d'Ariste' and wrote partial defenses against Locke and Du Tertre. (See the Bibliography below for further details.) Leibniz's endorsement of Malebranche was never unqualified and frequently was predicated upon an eccentric interpretation. He was not, therefore, a 'malebranchiste'.

10.	Foucher wrote of Leibniz's New System:

> It seems to me, in fact, that this system is hardly any more advantageous than that of the Cartesians [occasionalists] and, if we are right in rejecting their system because of its useless supposition that God bears in mind the movements He Himself produces in bodies and produces thoughts that correspond to these movements in the mind as well...will it not be relevant to ask you why God is not content simply to produce the thoughts and modifications of the mind...without there being useless bodies that the mind can neither move or know? (Gerhardt, C.I. ed., *Philosophische Schriften von G.W. Leibniz*, Berlin, 1875-90 : i 426).

11.	In this I agree with McCracken (see *Malebranche and British Philosophy*, p. 193) against those who suspect Collier of plagiarism. It is pertinent to note that there are a number of striking similarities between Leibniz's philosophy and that of Berkeley which could similarly be due to their common debt to Malebranche rather than to plagiarism on Berkeley's part.

12.	See Gerdil's works in the Bibliography. He, like many others, misunderstood Locke in taking him for a materialist.

13.	For the literature on Malebranche in nineteenth century French and Italian philosophy see the Bibliography by Gregor Sebba.

14. Bossuet, one of Malebranche's most powerful adversaries, is said to have written the words 'pulchra, nova, falsa' on his copy of the *Traité de la Nature et de la Grâce*. For an account of Bossuet's orthodox reaction against and Voltaire's defence of Malebranche's volonté génerale, see Riley (Patrick), *The General Will before Rousseau* (Princeton University Press, 1986): Ch. 2 and pp. 228-30 respectively. Professor Riley has incorporated some part of his account of the debate about Malebranche's 'general will' in Chapter 5 below, especially sections 3-5.

15. A seminal work on this aspect of Malebranche's influence and historical significance is Ferdinand Alquié's *Le cartésianisme de Malebranche*.

16. See Locke's 'Examination', Sections 11 and 16.

17. In his 'Reflections on the Doctrine of a Single Universal Spirit' of 1702, Leibniz makes this observation:

> Spinoza, who recognises only a single substance, is not far from the doctrine of a single universal spirit, and even the Neo-Cartesians, who hold that only God acts, affirm it, seemingly unawares. (Loemker (Leroy E.) trans., *Gottfried Wilhelm Leibniz: Philosophical Papers and Letters*, 2nd edition (Dordrecht: D. Reidel, 1969): 554.)

18. See the Bibliography under 'De Mairan' in the section on 'Malebranche and his Contemporaries'.

19. See the Bibliography under 'Malebranche and Eighteenth Century French Philosophy' below, p. 54, especially the works by Alquié, Acworth and Riley.

2　Bishop Pierre-Daniel Huet's Remarks on Malebranche

RICHARD H. POPKIN

Pierre-Daniel Huet, 1630-1721, who became the Bishop of Avranches, was one of the most severe critics of Cartesianism. He published some works on the subject, and left many many unpublished works. Among the latter are his marginal notes in his copies of various Cartesian writings, including his notes in his copy of Nicolas Malebranche's *De la Recherche de la Verité*.

Huet's library of over 8,000 volumes, was one of the largest of his time. He left it to the Jesuits, in whose premises in Paris he spent his last years. They gave it to the Royal Library, and it is now considered one of the basic collections of the Bibliothèque Nationale of Paris. (Huet's name is inscribed in marble as one of the original donors.) The volumes come with Huet's coat of arms. Only some of them have been separated from the general collection, and placed in the Salle de la Réserve.[1]

Two such items are Rés. R. 1925 (1) and Rés. R. 1926, volumes I and III of Malebranche's *Recherche de la verité*, 1674-75 edition. (The second volume is not in the catalogue. I was told years ago by a librarian, when working on Huet's marginalia, that various volumes of the Huet collection had been stolen, and sometimes came up for sale on the Paris quais. I was further told that the Bibliothèque Nationale had bought back several of the Huet items. After I heard this, I looked on the quais, and bought an item from the Huet collection, with his coat of arms. It has no marking indicating that it was ever part of the Bibliothèque Nationale collection.)

Huet marked up his volumes, and wrote detailed criticisms, comments and evaluations.[2] Some of this was presumably used in his writings. His discussion of Malebranche begins on the front fly-leaf, where he put down a quite strong critique and condemnation. He began, "Beaucoup de penetraõn dans cet ouvrage, beaucoup de discernement, beaucoup de meditaõn & de reflexion. Une eloquence masle, vive, riche, noble." Having said all of these nice things, Huet then turned to what was wrong. "Mais tout cela est corrumpu par trop de presomtion, de fierté, & de hardiesse. L'Auteur ne respecte pas mesme la religion, qu'il [blesse] si inconsiderement par ses paradoxes touchant le peché originel l'essence des corps et d'autres matieres, qu'il y a suject de [s]'estonner, que les Theologiens ne l'ayent encore censuré. Il meprise toutes les sciences qui luy manquent: & il luy en manque beaucoup, & presq~ toutes; hormis peutestre quelque teinture de Geometrie et d'Algebre, & de la Phtie [Philosophie] de Des Cartes, dont il est partisan aveugle, & quelque lecture de St. Augustin." Having pointed out Malebranche's limits, Huet went on to comment, "Foibles secours pour parvenir a la connoissance de la Verité, & pour bien traitter le Philosophie, qui estant selon la definition ordre la connoissance des choses divines & humaines demande un scavoir fort estendu." In fact, he continued, "Ses meditations, au lieu de la guerir de ses prejugez, et l'armer contre les vraysemblances selon le precepte de Descartes, luy ont fait prendre les visions extravagantes, des conjectures folles, et des suppositions bien plus incertaines q~ celles qu'il combat, po [pour] des veritez; pensant q~ l'air hautain et decisif dont il les avance, tiendroit lieu de raison, qu'il se feroit croire par les injures, qu'il en seroit quitte põ dire comme il fait si souvent, que ses opinions ne peuvent estre contestées que par des gens sujets aux impressions des sens & de l'imagination, abandonnez aux prejugez & aveugles aux lumieres de l'entendement."

To make the point more strongly, Huet remarked, "Avec quelle hauteur, et quel mepris n'a t'il pas répondu à l'Auteur de la Critique, hoe [homme] d'un esprit moderé, & dont il avoit esté traitté avec beaucoup d'honesteté.β Il [Malebranche] se plaint de ses railleries, luy qui n'employe souvent a ce seul moyen põ se debarasser des obiections, & po se defendre. Il se mocque de luy avoir cité Parmenide, Protagore, d'autres Phtes [Philosophes] anciens, croyant cacher son ignorance sous un mepris fastueux de toute sorte d'erudition. Il se plait de ses raisonnemens figurez, luy qui use si souvent d'apostrophes, plus propres a un sermon, qu a un traité de Phtie." Then Huet gave as examples "*Pauvre Caton* & c" and listed the pages where this occurred. "Tom.1. p. 28. Tom. 2. p. 156. 158. 160. 336." Next, "*Corps, esprits*, & c." Then Huet said nastily, "Il croi[r]oit prescher qd[quand] il declaimoit si pathetiquement contre les femmes qui decouvert leur sein: & il croi[r]oit enseigner la Theologie, qd po resoudre ses problemes il avoit si souvent recours a la volonté de Dieu, et aux causes surnaturelles." As a sort of summation of his evaluation of Malebranche's text, Huet then asserted, "Beaucoup de verbiage, de paroles inutiles, et de repetitions. Beaucoup de digressions affectées po avoir occasion d'estaler[?] ses opinions sur plusieurs questions disputées par. Mr. Descartes. Peu d'ordre, peu de methode; laquelle s'il iust apprise d'Aristote, sans dechaisner contre luy avec tant de fureur, il eust sceu diviser et definir; ce qui est si necessaire a un Philosophe, et qu'il a ignoré."

Starting from the preface, Huet marked up the text, putting marginal indications, underlinings, and page references to other texts. A complete understanding of Huet's reaction to reading Malebranche's *Recherche*, should involve noting all of these marks. Of course, the marks themselves do not indicate Huet's approval or disapproval. That has to be guessed at from other materials. Therefore, here I will only mention those places where Huet added some comment or commentary. These provide an illuminating enough judgment by Huet of Malebranche's great effort.

In the first chapter, [p. 14], Huet marked a passage and pointed out that Malebranche said the opposite on pp. 12 and 16. The text underlined on p.14 says, "que dans l'estat où nous sommes, nous ne connoissons les choses que imparfaitment..." Huet noted that two pages earlier and two pages later Malebranche had claimed that in the state in which we find ourselves, we often evidently see truth without any reason to doubt them.

On p. 24, Huet underlined Malebranche's statement that "il faut se soumettre également à la foy & à l'evidence", and "En un mot pour estre fidele il faut croire aveuglement, mais pour estre Philosophe il faut voir evidemment." Next to the first remarks, Huet wrote "Impie dictum", a comment that is repeated quite a few times throughout the text. Here, of course, is a central difference between Malebranche's rationalism and Huet's sceptical fideism. For Huet, any attempt to base religious knowledge on rational evidence, or to measure it by rational criteria, was impious, and threatened to cast religion in doubt. In Huet's sceptical treatise, *Traité de la foiblesse de l'esprit humain*, he made complete scepticism about all kinds of knowledge, the antecedent step to becoming a true believer. The battle between Huet's sceptical fideism, and Malebranche's rational theology goes on, as we shall see, throughout the annotations of the *Recherche*.

Other themes that begin to appear in the next few pages are to point out the sceptical implications, the confusions, and the unreported sources of what Malebranche was saying. When Malebranche commented about his method that if one could only act when one was entirely sure of success, one would often lose the chance to proceed, Huet said "Maxime Sceptique".

On the same page [25] where Malebranche declared that one should not absolutely scorn probabilities, "parce qu'il arrive ordinairement que plusiers estant jointes ensemble ont la mesme force pour convaincre que des demonstrations tres-evidentes." Huet coldly marked this, and wrote "Source d'erreur",

On the next page Huet marked Malebranche's effusive praise of his hero, "Descartes a découvert en trente années plus de veritez, que tous les autres Philosophes." Considering Huet's extremely negative view about Cartesian philosophy, as stated in his *Censura*, he must have been in a rage when he saw this.

A few pages later, in chap. iv, [33], Huet wrote after Malebranche had said, "La beauté de la justice ne se sent pas, la bonté d'un fruit ne se connoist pas", "L'un et l'autre est faux."

A different kind of fault finding occurs in the next chapter, v, [40] where Huet is happy to point out that Malebranche's discussion "Des erreurs de la veue au regard de l'entendue" has been taken from that of M. Pascal, whom Huet read with extreme care, and annotated his copy.[4]

In this chapter, Malebranche argued that God can always make smaller things, and hence, there must be infinitely small things. On p.41, Huet wrote, "On n'est pas obligé de croire q: Dieu ait fait tout ce qu'il a pu faire."

In the next chapter, vi, Huet took basic issue with Malebranche's notion of natural judgments. Huet underlined Malebranche's claim "ils sont naturels à l'homme" and wrote "Ils sont acquis par usage, et sont habituels, et non pas naturels."[56]. In the next section Huet challenged one of Malebranche's examples of natural judgments, and wrote "c'est à cause de la refraction, et non põ la raison qu'il allegue, qui est très fausse."[57]

Huet continued sniping at Malebranche's theory of natural judgment. On p.66, where Malebranche used the phrase "geometrie naturelle", Huet wrote "habituelle". A few pages later, he challenged Malebranche's explanation of how we know distances, insisting that the judgment of distance "est autre chose que cette veüe." [72]. On the next page, where Malebranche sought to explain why the moon seems larger when it rises, Huet wrote, "Tout ce raisonnement, et ce qu'il dit contre les refractionms est tres fausse." [73]

The next several entries deal with Huet's attack on Malebranche's explanation of the physics of seeing, Huet insisting that "Les couleurs ne se peignent point sur le nerf optiq; mais sur le retine, ou plutost sur la cloroide." [88] This point is made again on p. 111.

In the course of Malebranche's discussion of sense experience, Huet developed a challenge, first commenting that Malebranche confused sweetness with "l'agreeable. Tout le monde aime l'agreeable, mais tout le monde n'aime pas le doux." [101] The point in this criticism comes out in chapter XVI, where after saying that Malebranche's explanation of our feeling of pleasure and pain "Cela est tres faux:" [122], Huet pointed out that Malebranche's error is that he did not believe these sensible feelings were in the soul. "La source de leurs erreurs, c'est qu'ils croirent q: le corps n'estoit point une partie de l'homme, mais que l'ame seule estoit l'homme." [122]

In chapter XIX, sec. 3, Malebranche discussed why people have doubts, and had said that "Les Academiciens, & les Athées" doubt "par emportement & par brutalité." Huet testily commented "l'Auteur fait bien voir par ces paroles qu'il ne connoist pas la doctrine des Academiciens", which had just been exposited by Huet's friend and Malebranche's opponent, Simon Foucher. [134]

In the next part, Huet sought to show that Malebranche's views were theologically unsound. Where Malebranche had said that "la regne de la concupiscence" is what is called original sin in children, and actual sin in free men, Huet pointed out "D'ou il s'ensuit q le baptisme est inutile, puisq la concupiscence regne encore, après qu'on la receu." [172, misnumbered 272]

In Livre II, Part II, there are quite a few markings on passages. The first sizeable comment is on Malebranche's discussion of hieroglyphics. Huet put down his opinion on this topic which was much commented on at the time, "Les lettres et les Hieroglyphiques ont egalement un rapport immediat au sens car coe en voyant un certain Hieroglyphe, il me donne par exemple l'idée d'une maison, ainsi en voyant cette figure A. elle me donne l'idée du son qu'on fait en prononcant A." [203]

A curious quibble appears in chap. VI, in a comment on Malebranche's saying that it is useless to know what Aristotle believed about the immortality of the soul, although it is very useful to know that the soul is immortal. Huet did not defend Aristotle, but rather defended the value of knowing what Aristotle said, because, "La doctrine d'Aristote estant receüe dans les Escholes, mesme par autorité publiq. et par police, il est utile et necessaire de connoistre ses opinions." [217] This in no way endorses Aristotle's views, but shows the prudential value in knowing them.

In chap. IX, sec. III, where Malebranche attacked those who discover in Srcripture what the Holy Ghost has not said, Huet noted "Tract. Theologico. pol. cap. 14, p. 166 & seq." as well as one of Descartes's letters. [243] Huet was concerned with Spinoza's Bible criticism very soon after the *Tractatus* came out. Huet's critique of Spinoza was significant in the late seventeenth century.

In Part III, chap. I, sec. 1, when Malebranche said "Ces liens naturels, qui nous sont communs avec les bestes consistent dans une certaine disposition du cerveau", Huet underlined the last phrase, and announced "Il revient aux qualitez occultes." [250]

In chapter III, Huet carried on about the merits of Tertullian versus those of Malebranche. He ridiculed Malebranche's views about Seneca and Cato. He criticized Malebranche's discussion about pedantry. And then Huet turned for the rest of this book to attacking Malebranche's views about scepticism.

In dealing with chapter V, Huet said that Malebranche used terms equivocally [291]. He observed that when Malebranche said

"Toutes les creatures ont une obligation essentielle de tourner les esprits de ceux, qui les veulent adorer". Huet wrote "Il confond l'estime et l'adoraõn." [292] A few pages later on when Malebranche attacked the Academic sceptics, and said that one could convict them of being the most ignorant of men, Huet wrote, "Faux argument qui roule sur l'ambiguité du mot *savoir* ." Then when Malebranche continued saying that there is an essential difference between knowing and doubting, and if the Academics say what they think when they assert that they know nothing, one can say that they are the most ignorant of men, Huet replied, "Cõ si les Academiciens, lors qu'ils disent qu'ils ne savent rien, avoüent q; les autres hommes sceussent quelq chose." Then when Malebranche went on to explain why the Academics reject everything, namely "pour se faire passer pour esprits forts", Huet rebutted "c'est donc aussi p(our) passer p(our) esprit fort que l'Auteur aprés des Cartes a dit qu'il fallait se defaire de ses prejugez et apprendre a douter". So, Malebranche would also become a sceptic. All of this appears on p. 298.

In the last chapter of this book of the *Recherche*, Malebranche described someone who "croit voir la nuit des choses qui ne sont point, & qui estant réveillé ne peut discerner les songes des pensées qu'il a eües pendant le jour", Huet marked the passage, and wrote triumphantly, "Donc l'evidence est egale; donc l'evidence n'est pas une regle certaine de verité." So the Cartesian criterion of truth cannot apply. Malebranche then went on to explain that the principal thing which stops us from taking our dreams for realities is that we cannot connect our dreams with things we have done during the night, Huet referred to a text in Descartes' *Meditations*, and wrote "Si on songe donc des choses qui se puissent lier avec des choses de la veille, il n'y aura plus de distinction." [305] Again the criterion would be inapplicable. Lastly Huet wrote off Malebranche's discussion about demons as just "Verbiage".

Book III, chapter I deals with thought and "esprit". Huet underlined Malebranche's statement that "l'essence de l'esprit ne consiste que dans la pensée", and criticized it by saying that "S'il prend la pensée p(õ) la faculté de penser, cela est vray: mais non, s'il la prend p(our) l'action de penser." [312]

In the second chapter, Huet marked several sentences dealing with our ability to comprehend the divisibility of matter, and stressed Malebranche's admission that all of the objections on the subject cannot be resolved. [323]

In the third section of this chapter, Malebranche discussed our limited ability to understand the articles of Faith and the Mystery of the Trinity. He said that the objections that can be offered "sont si fortes, qu'il n'est pas possible d'en donner des solutions claires, évidentes, & qui ne choquent en rien nostre foible raison, parce qu'en effet ces mysteres sont incomprehensibles". Huet offered his defence,

"ces mysteres sont au dessus de la raison, mais ils ne la choquent pas."
[326].

There are no comments, but only occasional markings, until
Book III, Part II, chap. II, where Huet wrote, "Il suppose qu'il n'y a
point de vuide". [349]. On the next page where Malebranche
discussed points, Huet declared, "Le mot de point est equivoque; il se
prend põ un point mathematiq; et põ un fort petit espace. Or il n'y
point d'inconvement que toutes ces espaces se trouvent en un fort petit
espace". [350]

In the next paragraph Huet went on to say that Malebranche
was contradicting himself in dealing with tiny parts. Huet pointed out
that Malebranche had offered different explanations earlier, such as
that a grain of sand contains as many parts, although proportionally
smaller, than the whole earth. Huet criticized the next paragraph
concerning how we see geometrical shapes. Huet insisted that we do
not see circles and squares, but only shapes that resemble them. [350-
51]

In the next chapter, Huet disputed Malebranche's claim about
the nature of ideas, and wrote "absolum faux". [353]

Chapter VI, on seeing all things in God, brought out a great
deal of opposition from Huet. He marked the first paragraph, where
Malebranche said that he was going to show the dependence minds
have on God in all their thoughts. Huet listed two authorities, St.
Thom. Part 1, Quest. 84, art. 5, and Jamblich, de myster sist. 3, chap. 3,
p. 62. Then in another ink, (indicating an addition at a different time,
perhaps) Du Hamel, De consensu veter. et Nov. Philosoph Lib. 1, cap.
2, p.26.

At the bottom of the page, running on to the next page, Huet
wrote in Latin giving the views of Henry of Ghent, Scotus, Joh. Fr.
Picus, Examine Vanit. doctrin gentium, and quoted from that
Renaissance sceptical work. On the top of the next page, Huet cited
Augustine's Confessions, Book XII, chap. 25, Thomas, and Proclus,
De anime et Daemone. [365-66]. Huet seemed to believe he had to
line up a great many Christian and pagan authorities against this
central thesis of Malebranche. It is interesting that Huet, a Christian
fideist in all of his writings, appealed to St. Thomas.

A few pages later on, when Malebranche claimed that the proof
of the existence of God that is "la plus belle, la plus relevée, la plus
solide, & la premiere (all underlined by Huet), is that based on the our
idea of infinity, Huet commented "c'est la preuve de Descartes, qui est
très defecteuse". [369] A couple of lines later, Malebranche said, "Car
nous concevons l'estre infini de cela seul, que nous concevons l'estre
sans penser s'il est fini, ou infini". [369]. A couple of lines later,
malebranche said, "Car nous concevons l'estre infini de cela seul, que
nous concevons l'estre sans penser s'il est fini, our infini." Huet
responded, "Il confond l'estre infini avec l'estre indefini." [369]

16

Huet marked many of the key statements in the next chapters, but did not write anything until chapter VIII, sec. 2, where Malebranche argued that everything is either a being or a manner of being. Extension is not a manner of being, ... Huet wrote "on le nie. Autre chose est l'étendue; autre chose est un chose estendue. La matiere est une chose, ou un estre estendu. L'estendue est une maniere d'estre de la chose estendue. De plus son argument n'est pas en forme, et ne conclud pas; L'estendue est un estre; la matiere est un estre; Donc l'estendue est la matiere. S'il avoit autant leu Aristote q: Des Cartes il ne raisonnement pas ainsi." Right after this, Huet underlined "cependant on la conçoit fort facilement toute seule", and declared "c'est ce qu'on nie. On concoit un estre estendu, mais non pas l'estendue toute seule." [389] On the next page he repeated the contention that the Cartesian view that one can conceive of extension by itself. He said, "faux, mais bien avec quelq chose estendue." [390]

Huet continued his attack on the Cartesian notion of extension in the next couple of pages. In reference to a remark of Malebranche's, he wrote, "il se dit tres veritablement, car l'etendue ne peut subsister sans sujet, non plus q: la divisibilité, l'impenetrabilité, &c." Then, contra Malebranche, Huet insisted that "On ne cherche point de sujet en une chose qui subsiste par elle mesme. La matiere subsiste par elle mesme mais non pas l'estendue". [391]

Next when Malebranche started dealing with how one reconciles the Cartesian theory of matter with Church doctrine concerning Transsubstantiation, Huet marked the line "les manieres dont on explique les mysteres de la foy ne sont pas de foy" and underlined the one on p. 393 where Malebranche said "il suffit de tenir le dogme de la Transsubstantiation, sans en vouloir expliquer la maniere." Huet fiercely announced "C'est condamner la Concile de Trente, avec S. Thomas, et les autres Scholastiques." (Of course, when Huet stated his Christian fideism later on, he held that religion was accepted on faith, and not on reason, evidence, or even probabilities. In fact, when Huet was Bishop of Avranches, he was asked to look into the views of a Jesuit at Caen who held that there was no evidence of the truth of the Christian religion, and that of all the religions of the world, Christianity was the least probable. Huet reported that he spoke with the Jesuit, and found that he held the same views, *since* Christianity is a matter of faith alone.)[5]

In chap. IX, sec. 4, Huet criticized Malebranche's claim that "il semble que Dieu ne nous cache point ses ouvrages, & qu'il nous en auroit donné quelque idée", and wrote "Maxime tres fausse et contraire a la parole de Dieu." [397] Huet marked several passages in the rest of this chapter.

In chap. XI, Huet rejected Malebranche's attack on libertines and vicious people as always opinionated, and declared that "On n'est opinastre que qd on soustient une mauvaise opinion avec perservance, sans voulior reconnoistre, ou se rendre à la raison" something which Huet implied was the case with Cartesians. [415] There are some underlinings in the Conclusion of the First Three Books.

On the back flyleaf, there are some notes about pages on which certain topics appear. Then Huet said, "Des Cartes, lettre Tom, 2, p. 178, n'approuve pas qu'on mesle la Phtie avec la Religion". A quote is then given from St. Thomas, 1 quaest. 17, a.2, and a list of references to Augustine, Eusebius, Arnobius, Seneca, and to an article in the *Bibliotheque universelle*, Tome 6, p. 434, which says that "Regius dit que nous voyons les choses en Dieu."

As mentioned at the beginning of this study, the second volume of Huet's copy of Malebranche's *Recherche* is missing. In the third volume, with the "eclaircissements" there are a fair amount of markings and underlinings of statements that Huet disagreed with in the Eclaircissement on Book I, chap. 10. Towards the end of this section where Malebranche tried to explain why we should believe some things when we have no proof, Huet snapped, "Il faut donc adjouster foy aux choses dont nõ n'avons point d'idée claire et distincte." A sentence later, when Malebranche said that all natural judgment comes from God, Huet wrote "Cela se peut dire des faussetez coe [comme?] des verités." [72] He marked several passages in the rest of this section.

In the following sections, there are many markings and underlining, but practically no marginalia until the "Objection contre art. 17 et seq." Huet had marked the passage, "enfans dans le Batême sont justifiez par des mouvemens actuels de leur volonté vers Dieu", and declared "Cette opinion est un Lutheranisme" and gave references to texts in Cardinal Bellarmine, and Besanus. [165] On the next page, Huet marked a line about the prejudice that holds that children do not think in their mother's womb. This got Huet upset, and he wrote, "On ne doit point appeller prejugé qui est fondé sur de tres bonnes raisons, savoir sur l'imbecillité des organes, et sur l'experience: car on ne voit aucune marque exterieure q; les enfans pensent de la maniere q; pretend l'Auteur. Et qd ce seroit un prejugé, il veut destuire par une conjecture, qui n'est fondée sur aucune raison". Then he referred to two letters of Descartes. [166]

In the Eclaircissement X sur la nature des idees, Huet marked the passage where Malebranche said, that he knew by experience that there are many persons who are not capable of enough strong attention "pour concevoir les raisons que j'ai données de ce principe", Huet sneered, "Toujours prest a se vanger par des inures et des mepris de ceux qui ne le croyent pas". [188] A few pages later, when Malebranche said that "Il n'y a personne qui ne convienne que tous les hommes sont capables de connoître la verité", he announced proudly "Les Academiciens et les Pyrrhoniens n'en conviendront pas." [192] Then Huet underlined the news that "tout esprit" necessarily sees that

2+2=4, and wrote, "Il ne le voit pas necessairement s'il est vray. selon M. des Cartes que 2 fois 4 ne fussent pas 8". [194] and cites what Malebranche had said in the Eighth Eclaircissment, response to first objection, namely that Descartes had said in the response to the sixth objections that that God could make it such that 2 times 4 was not 8, and that the three angles of a triangle were not equal to two right angle. [107] Huet had underlined this.

Two pages later on, where Malebranche had said "la raison que l'homme consulte est infinie", Huet wrote, "Cette infinité pretendue peut autant venir de la foiblesse de l'esprit, que de la nature de la raison". [196] And a few pages later on, when Malebranche declared that "On appercoit au contraire d'une simple vüe & avec évidence, que la nature des nombres & des idées intelligibles est immuable, nécessaire, indépendante", Huet rebutted, "Il pose põ raison ce qui est en question". [200] Huet marked and underlined quite a few passages in the rest of this chapter.

In the next part, the objections "Contre ce qui a été dit, qu'il n'y a que Dieu qui nous éclaire...", where Malebranche said "Il vaut mieux être son maître à soi-même, que de chercher un maître parmi des créatures qui ne nous valent pas", Huet wrote "coe [comme] si le corps n'estoit pas une partie de nŝ mesme." [226] A couple of pages later Malebranche said, "l'ordre aimable par ses exemples, la lumière visible par un corps qui en diminue l'éclat". Huet snarled, "Figures oratoires, de nul Usage en Philosophie". [228]

There are quite a few markings and underlinings throughout the rest of the book, but only a few minor writings. In the "Reponse a une autre preuve", Huet underlined "J'avoüe qu'il ne faut pas recourir à Dieu ou à la cause universelle, lorsqu'on demande la raison des effets particuliers", and wrote nastily "Et c'est pourtant ce qu'il fait souvent". [337]

In the 15th Eclaircissement, in the Reponse, Huet underlined Malebranche's claim that "Car les Livres Saints n'ont pas été faits pour les Theologiens de ce tems-ci:mais pour le Peuple Juif", Huet declared "Falso et impie dictum". [386]

On the back flyleaf Huet just noted what was on a few pages.

Huet's remarks about Malebranche rehearse many of the points he later made in his published critiques of Cartesianism. He was so opposed that he criticized Malebranche from many points of view. Sometimes he was a sceptic, either an Academic or a Pyrrhonian, sometimes he was a traditionalist, sometimes he was a horrified Catholic, sometimes he was a commonsense scientist. The net effect of the material above does not in itself make up a consistent or complete criticism of Malebranche. But, it does indicate the reaction of the most important French sceptic of the time (who was then a friend, and defender, of Simon Foucher, the first critic, and critic from a sceptical stance). Huet hit upon many of the main points that were to

19

become the centrer of discussion between Malebranche and his opponents. And Huet was able to enlarge upon his critique of Cartesianism as a method, a philosophy, and a theology. Studying Huet's marginalia here, and in other Cartesian works, as well as his interfoliated notes in his critical works against Cartesianism, would give a fuller picture of what he was doing.

Two of the most interesting critics of Cartesianism were Gassendi and Huet. The former is beginning to get the serious study he deserves. Huet, possibly because he wrote so much, and because so much remains unpublished, has not been too well examined. He was a more astute thinker than Simon Foucher (if R. A. Watson will permit my saying so). He was extremely well read in traditional and contemporary philosophy. He was aware of the implications of various doctrines. And he read new thinkers as their books appeared. So, his reaction to Malebranche, as well as his reaction to Pascal, Spinoza and many others, is interesting to observe. It gives us a lively testimony to what was happening in the Republic of Letters at the time, from an important observer. Like Leibniz, he reads almost everything, knew almost everyone, and was not reticent about giving his views. He interpreted what was occuring from a sceptical point of view, as well as that of a Christian fideist. (And I think the marginal notes eliminate any plausibility to the suggestion that he was not a sincere believer.) The Malebranche notes were written fairly early in his career, before he had become a priest. He was at the time teacher to the Dauphin, and a leading figure in Paris intellectual salons. In the notes he was talking to himself, and so, not advancing views that could convince others of his purported sincerity. He was just expressing his private reaction to reading Malebranche's first publication. In so doing, he read it as anti-Cartesian, as a complete sceptic, and as a defender of modern science and fidestic Christianity, all views that he was to develop much more completely in later years.

Notes

1.   On Huet's career, see Léon Tolmer, *Pierre-Daniel Huet, (1630-1721, Humaniste-Physicien*, (Bayeux: Colas 1949)

2.   On this, see Richard H. Popkin, "The Marginalia and Correspondence of Pierre-Daniel Huet, Bishop of Avranches", *American Philosophical Society Yearbook*, 1957, pp. 364-366.

3.   This is Simon Foucher, author of *Critique de la Recherche de la Verité*, Paris 1675. Foucher at the time was a friend of Huet's.

20

4. I will discuss Huet's annotations in his copy of Pascal's *Pensées*, in a future study.

5. All the details on this appear in the Carteggio Huet, Bibioteca Laurenziana, Florence, Ashburnham Ms. 1866.

3.   Foucher's Mistake and Malebranche's Break: Ideas, Intelligible Extension and the End of Ontology

RICHARD A. WATSON

What is an idea? What is intelligible extension? Until about the middle of the latter half of the seventeenth century, Western philosophers generally seemed to think that the answers to such philosophical questions, the solutions to philosophical problems, and philosophical explanations had to be given in terms of ontological models. In this paper I focus on a dividing point. Simon Foucher's criticisms of the Cartesian way of ideas, and particularly the question of intelligible extension, led Malebranche to make one of the first modern breaks with the traditional substance/property ontology. Thereafter, the way was open for philosophers to consider questions about ideas and intelligibility as purely epistemological issues, and eventually to deny that "What is an idea?" could or should have an ontological answer.[1]

Simon Foucher (1644-1696) was a late seventeenth century French sceptic, remarkable as the friend who first drew the monadology from Leibniz, and as the enemy who first attacked Malebranche's occasionalism. His pivotal position in Modern philosophy is further assured by his having made one of the most influential mistakes in the history of philosophy. It would not be too much to say that Foucher's mistake is the key to most of Anglo-American empirical philosophy from his day until now. Foucher's mistake was to take the distinction Descartes made between intelligible and sensible qualities of material things (what Locke later called primary and secondary qualities) to be a distinction between some sensible qualities and other sensible qualities.[2]

22

Foucher says that the Cartesians face a dilemma. They contend that certain qualities such as tastes and sounds and colours are not properties of material objects, but other qualities such as size and shape and motion are. But because the shape and colour of a material object appear to be in the same place, if the colour is a sensation or property of the mind and not of the material object, then the shape is also, *or*, if the shape is a property of the material object, so is the sensation or colour. There is nothing, Foucher insists, in our experience to distinguish the so-called intelligible ideas from sensations. He agrees that colour is a property of the mind. Thus, all ideas and sensations are sensible properties of the mind. Foucher's mistake - the assimilation of intelligible ideas to sensations - leads to the view that we have no direct knowledge of the external material world.

Descartes does say that both ideas and sensations are properties of the mind. He says some intelligible ideas represent material objects, but no sensations do (although sensations can indicate their presence). Against this position, Foucher argues by appealing to the epistemological likeness principle - that to represent an object, an idea must resemble that object. Because ideas and sensations are mental, they cannot resemble material things and thus cannot represent them. Thus again, on Descartes's view, we have no direct knowledge of matter.

Foucher's assimilation of ideas to sensations is based on quite a serious misunderstanding of Descartes. In the wax example of the second *Meditation*, Descartes says:

> But even as I speak, I put the wax by the fire, and look: the residual taste is eliminated, the smell goes away, the colour changes, the shape is lost, the size increases; it becomes liquid and hot; you can hardly touch it, and if you strike it, it no longer makes a sound.[3]

He goes on to say:

> So what was it in the wax that I understood with such distinctness? Evidently none of the features which I arrived at by means of the senses; for whatever comes under taste, smell, sight, touch or hearing has now altered - yet the wax remains.[4]

Descartes concluded that one knows of extension through an intuition of the mind by way of intelligible ideas, not through imagination or the senses, but through the faculty of reason. What one knows is intelligible extension, in contradistinction to the sensible extension that varies so radically in the experiment with the wax.

It is obvious that Descartes, as well as Foucher, recognizes that the extension we see is sensible, just as is the colour we see. Thus the first of Foucher's arguments is misdirected, and could be offered and taken seriously only by those who grossly misunderstand Descartes's conception of the intelligible (and innate) idea(s) of matter.

Foucher's second argument has more plausibility. Cartesian thoughts, including ideas and sensations, are ontologically properties of the mind. They are mental, and as such are entirely unlike the material. If resemblance is necessary between what represents and what is represented, then there can at least be no ontological resemblance between Cartesian ideas and material things. Foucher's argument is that if the Cartesians, as many of them seem to, agree that representation must be based on resemblance, and that this resemblance must be of an ontological kind, then mental ideas cannot represent material objects. But *are* ideas properties of the mind? Foucher and the Cartesians believe they are. To show one difficulty this raises, I now examine the notions of representation and of intelligible extension that appear in Descartes and Malebranche. This leads to the further question of whether or not ideas are properties at all.

In the wax example, Descartes indicates that while sensible extension is in the mind, the extension which is intelligible and which is known by way of ideas is not in the mind. This raises three questions:

1.   What is intelligible extension, i.e., is it matter?

2.   What are the ideas by which we know intelligible extension, i.e., are they properties of the mind?

3.   What is the relation between intelligible extension, the ideas of it, and matter, i.e., is this relation resemblance?

Cartesians explain the knowing process with an ontological model that is as central to Locke as it is to Descartes: the inherence relation of substance/property between a mind and an idea or a sensation is identical with the knowing relation of knower/known. It is assumed that the mind knows its own properties by direct acquaintance because it is in direct contact with them. Direct acquaintance = direct contact = a substantial mind having a property = a mind knowing an idea or a sensation. The unmediated *directness* of this contact assures the certainty of knowledge of ideas and sensations as such. On either Cartesian or Lockean grounds, the reason one knows ideas and sensations as they are is because they are ontologically direct properties of the mind.

The notion that direct acquaintance gives the mind certain knowledge of its object is crucial. The substance/property ontology that supports the direct acquaintance of a mind with its own ideas is the explanatory substructure that prevents Cartesian philosophers from breaking out of the circle of ideas. This ontological model confines

Locke also to direct knowledge only of ideas. One would like to have certain knowledge of the external world, but if this requires taking ideas to be something other than properties of the mind, then one runs the risk of losing even the certainty gained from the mind's direct acquaintance with ideas. Malebranche runs this risk. Berkeley, however, repeating Foucher's mistake of assimilating ideas to sensations, gives up any claim to knowledge of independent external material objects at all, settling for the immediately certain knowledge of sensible ideas.

Malebranche does not make Foucher's mistake. He does not assimilate ideas to sensations. But he does break with Descartes by abandoning the substance/property model of mind for ideas, although he keeps it for the relation between the mind and sensations. That is, Malebranche meets the epistemological challenge to knowledge of matter by saying that ideas are *not* modifications or properties of the mind, although sensations are. The sensations of wax are thus in the mind. But ideas are not properties of the mind, and thus we are not directly acquainted with them the way we are with sensations. What, then, are ideas? And how do ideas make things known? They are *in* God. As properties of God? No: God has no properties. Ideas are independent of substances. We know them directly because God shares his ideas with us, and through them we know material things. Malebranche says that we see all things in God. But this is as far as he goes by way of explanation. We know by way of independent, intelligible ideas that are not mental properties, but we are not told exactly what they are.

Does Malebranche think of ideas on a Platonic model, as eternal archetypes? If one takes this line of interpretation, then what is intelligible is each idea itself. Then to answer the three questions above, intelligible extension is an eternal archetype-idea independent of our minds that we know directly through God's illuminating or sharing it with us, and that gives us general knowledge of matter by resembling it as its archetype. But this is a far remove from the knowledge we were originally seeking. This model gives us knowledge of a perfect, eternal, intelligible extension and thus a general knowledge of matter, but no knowledge of particular bodies. We were trying to get out of the Cartesian circle of ideas to knowledge of the everyday material world, but have ascended instead to the Platonic heaven.

To attempt an escape from that mausoleum in the sky, I delay the question of what an idea is to consider now the question of what intelligible extension is. Commentators including Randall[5], Schrecker[6], Brunschvicg[7], Gouhier[8], Bergmann[9], and Bracken[10] suggest that what Descartes and Malebranche mean by intelligible extension is geometry, the axioms, I take it, of solid Euclidlean geometry. (Laporte takes important exception to this interpretation, and his two articles on intelligible extension in Descartes and Malebranche are worth careful study.)[11]

Let me say at the outset that I agree with Laporte[12] that if this is what Descartes and Malebranche mean, it is an enigma that they do not come right out and say so. Both are skilled mathematicians, and Descartes's discovery of analytic geometry is based on his understanding of the relational similarities between geometric figures and algebraic formulations. Perhaps Descartes and Malebranche do not say that intelligible extension just *is* the axiomatic system of geometry, because this is not exactly what they mean. But what they do mean is unclear.

The discussion involves three phrases: sensible extension, material extension, and intelligible extension. Are there then three sorts of extension? Remember that on Cartesian grounds we never have any direct acquaintance with material extension. Our understanding of it must be mediated by something with which we do have direct acquaintance. We have direct acquaintance with sensible extension, but sensible extension is said to be totally unlike material extension. This opens the possibility that there is something else with which we are directly acquainted by way of which we understand material extension. This something else could be called intelligible extension, and an obvious candidate for it is the set of axioms of solid Euclidian geometry. Intelligible extension could be just our ideas of geometry. (Note that I here set aside a possible Malebranchean answer that intelligible extension is a Platonic archetype, and in this Cartesian context I do not consider the notion that it is an Aristotelian-Thomistic form.)

While material extension may be intelligible because it is understood by way of geometric ideas, material extension itself - the Cartesian substance - must be something other than the set of geometric relations it exhibits. Of course Descartes says that so-called empty space is matter, and this might suggest that matter is a bare set of geometric relations (as Newton later said space is). But Descartes also says that we can know all about matter even when we do not know whether it exists, i.e., even if it did not exist. Thus matter must be something other than the set of relations by which we understand it, and, to the specific point, the set of relations must be something other than the matter it makes known. Descartes makes good the claim that we could know intelligible extension even if matter did not exist by exhibiting geometric relations in unextended, algebraic form. That an isomorphism of relations exists between algebraic and geometric representations is the key to how Descartes and Malebranche might take unextended mental ideas to represent material extension. They are ontologically unlike one another, but they can exhibit - isomorphically - the same set of relations.

26

To reach this denouncement, however, I must first give an exposition of the view that intelligible extension *is* the set of axioms and rules, the axiomatic system, of geometry. This interpretation incorporates a deductive model in Descartes's rationalistic physics.

Two versions can be proposed of the view that intelligible extension *is* a set of geometric axioms. A Spinozistic view is that the whole of matter, all of extension or space, is or embodies the set of axioms, while each individual material thing constitutes a theorem derivable from these axioms. The relation between each individual body and its properties is of the same deductive sort as that between matter and individual bodies.

This axiomatic interpretation seems to be a reasonable guess about Descartes's meaning when he says extension is intelligible. It is a rational, mathematical, and non-occult way of understanding the traditional view that a substance contains and generates its properties. One can say that the essence at least of material substance is intelligible if one thinks of it as a set of axioms that contains its own properties as axioms contain theorems. Material extension can be made intelligible by describing it analogically as a set of axioms because it has a structure isomorphic with the axioms of solid Euclidian geometry. One can also say that material extension is a substance that can be taken as the interpretation of a calculus or set of relations that also can be interpreted with the terms of solid Euclidean geometry.

Putting aside the question of what the calculus or set of relations is in itself, note that on this plan material extension is made intelligible, presumably in contradistinction to unintelligible sensible extension. But sensible extension *also* provides an interpretation, albeit perhaps a poor or rough one, for the calculus of solid Euclidean geometry.[13] This is an interpretation with which we are all familiar, one we learned in secondary school and the one architects use. *Sensible* extension is also intelligible on the axiomatic interpretation. This explains the fact that we *do* learn about material extension when we examine sensible extension. We may never know material extension directly, but we do know sensible extension directly, and because both exhibit the same relations - both are interpretations of the same calculus, the same model or set of relations - we can learn about material extension by examining sensible extension. Descartes does not say this, but his development of analytic geometry makes it plausible.

Both material extension and sensible extension are intelligible with relation to an axiomatic deductive calculus. But is intelligible extension *just* a set of axioms or relations? If one takes intelligible extension to be only a set of axioms, then two problems present themselves. First, what are these axioms? Are they Platonic entities? Are they descriptive of or do they refer to mathematical entities? I continue to try to keep my feet on the ground, but if I accept the notion that extension just *is* a set of axioms, I find myself ballooned once again to the Platonic heaven, with little hope of contacting matter.

Second, how can intelligible extension taken as a set of geometric relations be interpreted with matter? Descartes is concerned with the deductive model because of his desire to establish a rationalistic physics. The problem is that geometry is static and eternal, like God, whereas our world is dynamic and temporal.

It is not enough, then, to say that matter is a set of axioms and that individual bodies are theorems, or that matter and bodies can provide interpretations of a calculus. This tells us what shapes matter could take, and this is anything three-dimensional. It is like saying that in a block of marble there are an infinite number of statues. But the matter we are concerned to know about is divided into actual bodies, and these bodies are in motion. Norman Kemp Smith argues that the whole rationalist enterprise is necessarily doomed to failure because the eternal relations of logic cannot be used to represent the temporal relations in the world.[14] There is, however, a way to utilize logic or an axiomatic calculus as a representation of the temporal world. One adds a pragmatic element to the model (one calls in the demiurge).

Beyond pairing the axioms with matter and the theorems with individual bodies, we can coordinate the rules for deduction with the physical laws of nature, and the actual process of deducing with the temporal course of natural events. This provides a total interpretation not just of extension, but also of the dynamic material world, made intelligible with relation to an axiomatic system.

Again, this approach involves not merely interpreting the axioms as matter and theorems as individual bodies, but also interpreting the rules of deduction as the physical laws of nature, and the actual process of deducing theorems from axioms as the causal chain of natural physical events. In Cartesian terms, this is an exact explication of God in the role of both Prime Mover and Great Deducer. To understand God's ways with the material world, one understands the world as an operating axiomatic deductive system. But this is not to say that material extension *is* nothing but a set of axioms and rules in dynamic process.

I might give one word of caution. Even if we comprehended this system and had a Laplacean state description of it for a given time, we could deduce events, but not be certain that our descriptions would be true of the actual course of events. This is because just as an individual theorem is deducible in various ways from a set of axioms, so is it the case that a particular physical event can be the result of many different courses of events. And just as with the same rules from any set of axioms different theorems can be deduced, so is it the case that in accordance with the same laws of nature from any set of given physical circumstances various courses of physical events can proceed.

So even if we know all the laws of nature and that the course of events leading to the present situation in the physical world is deducible, we cannot thereby deduce with certainty which course got us to the present pass, because any number of deducible courses would get us here according to the laws of nature. And therefore, we cannot know which of the many possible future events will transpire, because many future courses of events are in accord with the laws of nature. All this goes to recommend the interpretation, because it is the case that our knowledge of the physical world is contingent in just this way.

Matter is intelligible on the deductive axiomatic model, but it is more than just a set of axioms. So we are still left with the question of what intelligible extension - the axiomatic model - *is*. But whatever the axiomatic model itself *is* (whatever a set of relations or a formal structure in itself - uninterpreted, unexhibited, or unembodied - *is*), and whether ideas are properties of the mind or Platonic or mathematical entities or something else, the model provides us with knowledge of material extension even though we do not know what the model is (it may not be *anything*). There *is* something similar between the model and matter - the relations exhibited in each. And because these relations are *also* exhibited in sensible extension, a tie is established between sensible and material extension. *Both* turn out to be intelligible on this account, and an explanation is thus provided for how we do learn about such properties of matter as size and shape through sense perception. One persuasive argument for this interpretation, then, is that is absolves Descartes of the absurdity of having to claim that sensible extension is not like real extension. Sensible extension is like real extension because they exhibit the same relations, just as algebraic formulae and plane figures do in analytic geometry.

But what *is* the mere set of relations in itself? What *is* intelligible extension contrasted both to material extension and to sensible extension? Can we say that the whole being of the set of relations is epistemological, that it is merely what makes material extension and sensible extension intelligible? This may be the right way out, but in the Cartesian context of providing explanatory ontological models, the question of what the set of relations is in itself and the perhaps equivalent question of what intelligible extension is in itself demand ontological answers.

To break out of this mold, let us return to Malebranche and again to the question: What is an idea? Malebranchean ideas are in God and in our minds not by way of being properties or modifications, but by way of being known. Like later positivists, Malebranche thus tries to restrict the discussion of ideas to their *epistemological* nature or function of representing objects, and he tries to avoid discussing their *ontological* nature or status, a question that Foucher believes must be answered to explain how ideas can represent their objects. Foucher insists that there must be an ontological model to explain the knowing process.

The causal and epistemological likeness principles seem as solid to Foucher as any principles can be other than the self-evident law of noncontradiction in mathematics. He simply cannot believe that Malebranche truly rejects them. He thinks Malebranche is saying that God miraculously bypasses the requirement of resemblance to get out of a Cartesian dualist dilemma. Surely Malebranche implicitly accepts the causal likeness principle - that interacting objects must be like one another - because his philosophy of occasionalism is a direct response to the impossibility of Cartesian mind-body interaction. Malebranche also implicitly accepts the epistemological likeness principle because his theory of ideas that are "in" God and "shared" by us is designed to get around the impossibility of Cartesian ideas representing bodies. And as Foucher points out, Malebranche's magic ideas and miraculous occasionalism are over-responses to the problem in the face of uncertainty about the essences of mind and matter that might after all be enough alike to support representative ideas and causal interaction. It is just at this precise moment in the history of philosophy that the very question itself - *What* is an idea? (What *is* intelligible extension?) - becomes suspect.[15] *Does* an idea *have* ontological status? If it is a property of a mind, ours or God's, then problems arise about its representative nature, its epistemological status. If it is a Platonic Idea, or a Malebranchean idea "in" God Who "shares" it with us, is it an independent substance? If it is different both from mind and matter, how could it be an archetype of - i.e., resemble - either one or the other? Just how does it make anything intelligible or known to us?

Neither Malebranche nor Descartes nor anyone else who asserts that ideas represent objects without resembling them knows how to defend the view that ideas then *can* represent objects or make them intelligible. Again the crucial question is: What is an idea? If it is not a property of a substance, and if it is not a substance itself, then what is it? Malebranche simply does not know. But - in a Cartesian context - what *can* an idea be if it is neither a property nor a substance? (It certainly cannot be a Thomistic substantial form.)

The notion that ideas represent by resembling their objects is now generally rejected as a Modern dogma.[16] Yet, the principle of representation by resemblance has never been abandoned in practice. Repeating Foucher's mistake, Berkeley and Hume assimilate Cartesian ideas to sense impressions (properties of the mind or independent momentary substances), atomic building blocks that are the ancestors of both the neutral monads of James and Russell and the sense data of Carnap and Wittgenstein. Hume talks of ideas that resemble impressions and Berkeley of ideas resembling other ideas.

30

Resemblance is the very foundation of Wittgenstein's *Tractatus* in which symbols are arranged in patterns isomorphic with facts. Of course that Ancient position is discredited by Wittgenstein himself in the *Investigations*, but what can either unreconstructed positivists or new Post-modernists say to Foucher's old question: What, then, *is* an idea? They say that the question does not make sense. It is a category mistake to ask it. Ideas are not anything.

The specific point I want to make is that the encounter between Malebranche and Foucher concerning ideas represents a temporal divide or turning point before which time the answers to questions about the representative nature of ideas and their epistemological status required ontological models. Malebranche and Foucher argue on the Ancient ground in which ideas have solid ontological being, but just because of that - at least in the Cartesian context - ideas begin to look incapable of carrying out their epistemological task of representing objects, of making them known. In the context of radical Cartesian dualism, and with the assumption that one can coherently deny the causal and epistemological likeness principles, Foucher's questions expose the total incapacity of the Cartesian model of substance philosophy to explain events of representation by ideas and of causal interaction between mind and body that obviously take place.

Malebranche - by overtly denying the causal and epistemological likeness principles - tries to blast his way out of the cage of substance philosophy in which Foucher has caught him.[17] But Foucher asks, if there is no causal interaction between mind and body, why does God make it appear that there is? Instead of miracles, surely a philosopher is required to provide a philosophical explanation, i.e., an ontological model that explains how mind and matter *do* interact, if not based on likeness then on some other principle. If Malebranche's ideas "in" God are not like either mental properties or material bodies, and if ideas do not have to resemble material bodies to represent them, then, you might hear Foucher shouting above the noise of collapsing foundations, what are these new ideas? Similarly, given his overt rejection of the epistemological likeness principle, Malebranche is surely required to offer an explanatory model that provides ontological ground for the representative nature of ideas. If representation is *not* based on resemblance between an idea and its object, what, then, *is* it based on?

Neither Malebranche nor Foucher saw that the Modern way out was to be an utter denial of the meaningfulness of the question "What is an idea?" taken as a demand to provide an ontological model that explains how representation can and does take place, and that the Modern answer to how causal interaction takes place was to be the rejection or at the very least the ignoring of the demand for an ontological explanatory model, but instead the provision of a Humean Godless and causeless version of Malebranchean occasionalism - a

31

description - not an explanation on metaphysical or ontological grounds, but a mere *description* of the course or sequence of events.

Now consider again the question of what *is* the set of relations in itself that is offered as intelligible extension. Just what is this idea that makes extension or matter intelligible? Perhaps the best answer is, after all, that it is a mathematical entity, that the set of relations we know as the axioms, rules, and theorems of solid Euclidean geometry subsist eternally in the Platonic heaven. Malebranche seems to imply this. But today geometry *itself* is presented as just one possible interpretation of that set of relations, which when uninterpreted, unexhibited, or unembodied becomes so abstract and empty as to be itself unintelligible in the sense of being inaccessible. Notice that while in Aristotelian terms, this set of relations would be a form that informs matter, it also begins to look like sheer potentiality or to have something in common with prime matter, or in comparison to more recent entities, to have the featureless aspect of bare particulars. But because it does inform content, it has to have features. And is not what has features something? But what? Does this set of relations actually have any ontological status at all? The current answer is no. The explanatory model itself neither exists nor subsists. It is that by which we know. It is solely epistemological. Thus it does not provide explanation by being an ontological model. The immediate claim is that ideas are not things of any sort. The underlying assumption is that ontology does not support epistemology as Foucher thought it should.

This is what I mean by "the end of ontology" in my title. Foucher asks questions in the Ancient tradition. He demands ontological models as philosophical explanations of how representation and causation take place. Malebranche gives answers that cannot possibly provide satisfactory ontological models of explanation. This makes Foucher satisfied that he has shown Malebranche's system to be as much a failure as Descartes's, and it drives Malebranche into total dependence on the adequate - overly adequate but densely opaque - ways of God. Not dependence on the *machinations* of God, mind you, no mechanical nor any other models of how representation and causal interaction can take place are provided, but merely the assurance that God can do what He will and is done.

Philosophers today have become fairly well adapted to the lack of ontological models of causation. Scientific description has replaced metaphysics. But, as I remark above, Wittgenstein in the *Tractatus* still works with a model in which representation is based on likeness in the form of isomorphic relations. His model of how symbols represent facts is based on the formal relations that play a role in the discussions of intelligible extension. And although Wittgenstein himself later denies that resemblance is the ground on which ideas represent their objects or symbols represent facts, and even though many philosophers since Descartes and Malebranche deny that likeness is required for representation and causal interaction, and despite the fact that many philosophers today deny that the question "What is an idea?" requires or even can have an answer in terms of an ontological model that shows or explains how and why an idea can and does represent its object, the demand that Foucher makes of Malebranche for an ontological model still seems cogent. If resemblance is not the ground of representation, then what *is*? Early positivists say that ideas are sets of relations. Later analysts say they are meanings, intentions, mental acts, or speech acts. But what are *they*? What is a meaning? The Ancient substance/property ontology once provided a solid ground for philosophical explanation, but is now seen to be insubstantial. The questions remain: What is an idea? What makes extension intelligible? If giving an ontological model does not provide an explanation for what makes it possible for us to know, then just how is it that we do know?

NOTES

1. For detailed documentation of background points made here, see Part Two, "The Downfall of Cartesianism", in Richard A. Watson, *The Breakdown of Cartesian Metaphysics*, Atlantic Highlands, Humanities Press International, 1987. I would now, as the present article shows, put much stronger emphasis on Foucher's demand for an ontological model on which to base philosophical explanation, and on the radical nature of Malebranche's attempt to avoid this demand, than I do in *Breakdown* .

2. Popkin, Richard H. "L'abbé Foucher et le problème des qualités premières," *Bulletin de la société d'étude du XVIIe siècle*, No. 33, 1957, pp. 633-647.

3. Descartes, René, *Meditations on First Philosophy* in *The Philosophical Writings of Descartes* translated by John Cottingham, Robert Stoothoff, and Dugald Murdoch, Vol. 2, Cambridge, Cambridge University Press, 1984, p. 20; *Oeuvres de Descartes* edited by Charles Adam and Paul Tannery, Vol. 7, p. 30.

4. Ibid.

5. Randall, John Herman Jr. "Religio Mathematici: The Geometrical World of Malebranche", *Studies in the History of Ideas*, Vol. 2, New York, Columbia University Press, 1925, pp. 185-218; *The Career of Philosophy: From the Middle Ages to the Enlightenment*, Vol. 1, New York, Columbia University Press, 1962, pp. 425-433.

6. Schrecker, Paul. "La méthode cartésienne et la logique", *Review Philosophique*, Vol. 123, 1937, pp. 336-367; "The Parallélisme théologico-mathematique chez Malebranche", *Révue Philosophique , Vol. 124, 1938, pp. 215-252.*

7. Brunschvicg, Léon *Les étapes de la philosophie mathématique des cartésiens.* 3rd edition. Paris: Presses Universitaires Françaises, 1947.

8. Gouhier, Henri. *La philosophie de Malebranche et son expérience religieuse*, 2nd edition, Paris, Libraire Philosophique J. Vrin, 1948.

9. Bergmann, Gustav. "Some Remarks on the Philosophy of Malebranche", *Review of Metaphysics*, Vol. 10, 1956, pp. 207-225.

10. Bracken, Harry. "Some Problems of Substance Among the Cartesians", *American Philosophical Quarterly*, Vol. 1, 1964, pp. 129-137.

11. Laporte, Jean. "La connaissance de l'étendue chez Descartes" pp. 11-36 and "L'étendue intelligible selon Malebranche" pp. 153-192 in *Études d' histoires de la philosophie française au XVIIe siècle*, Paris, Libraire Philosophique J. Vrin, 1951. See also P. E. Elungu, *Étende et connaissance dans la philosophie de Malebranche*, Paris, Libraire Philosophique J. Vrin, 1973; and Michael E. Hobart, *Science and Religion in the Thought of Nicholas Malebranche*, Chapel Hill, University of North Carolina Press, 1982.

12. Laporte, Jean. "L'étendue intelligible selon Malebranche", in *Études d' histoires de la philosophie française au XXVIe siècle*, Paris, Librairie Philosophique J. Vrin, 1951, p. 168.

13. See the discussion of visible extension in R. B. Angell, "The Geometry of Visibles", *Nous*, Vol. 8, 1974, pp. 87-117.

14. Smith, Norman Kemp. *Studies in the Cartesian Philosophy*, London, Macmillan, 1902, pp. 244 ff.

15. See also William Gottfried Leibniz, "What is an Idea?" in *Philosophical Papers and Letters* edited and translated by Leroy E. Loemker, Vol. 1, Chicago, University of Chicago Press, 1956, pp. 317-319; *Die Philosophischen Schriften von Gottfried Wilhelm Leibniz* edited by C. J. Gerhardt, Vol. 7, Berlin, Weidmannsche, 1875, pp. 256-264.

16. For example, in Richard Rorty, *Philosophy and the Mirror of Nature*, Princeton, Princeton University Press, 1979.

17. See Edwin B. Allaire, "The Attack on Substance: Descartes to Hume", *Dialogue*, Vol. 3, 1964, pp. 284-287.

34

4 The Malebranche-Arnauld Debate:[1] Philosophical or Ideological?[2]

HARRY M. BRACKEN

There should never have been a 'debate' over the controversy between Malebranche and Arnauld concerning 'representative ideas'.[2] Worse yet, many of the participants have been inclined to favour Arnauld's side and to treat it as philosophically superior. Such judgments are based on two mistakes: (1) a failure to take seriously an (the) essential element in Malebranche's philosophy and (2) a failure to see that the 'framework' within which Arnauld formulates his criticisms of Malebranche is totally incoherent. Thus understood, Arnauld's often heralded victory in the debate does not rest on a philosophical foundation. In fact, the dramatic quality which the debate undoubtedly possesses derives primarily from the vigour with which Malebranche and Arnauld attack one another. And the hostility they express is itself rooted in the French Catholic political warfare of the seventeenth century. Arnauld and the Port Royalists of the Jansenist persuasion saw in Cartesians, and especially in the Cartesians among the Oratorians, kindred theological spirits. But Malebranche's *Traité de la nature et de la grâce* (1680)[3] marks a clear break with Jansenism. Malebranche's effort to articulate his theological orthodoxy seems to be taken by Arnauld as something akin to betrayal.[4] Thus the so-called philosophical dispute occurs in a context of real political and theological conflict.

The sorts of philosophical difficulties with which I am concerned can be seen, for example, when John Yolton begins his philosophical analysis and historical characterization of 'perceptual acquaintance' with a brief survey of certain features of the scholastic tradition which, it is said, Descartes, Malebranche, Arnauld and Locke all inherit. Yolton writes: "The Aristotelian form is clearly the

35

ancestor of the seventeenth and eighteenth-century concept of ideas, certainly of the Cartesian version. Descartes' notion of the objective reality of ideas is a direct descendent of St Thomas's account, with borrowings from Aristotle."[5]   Briefly, Yolton contends that the celebrated theory of ideas yielded two very different doctrines: representative ideas versus direct realism. It is the direct realist option in Arnauld (and even in Locke!) which he wishes to recover, i.e. ideas seen as acts of understanding which directly relate minds to objects rather than as representative intermediary entities.

According at least to some interpreters of the Thomistic account,[6] the agent intellect abstracts the intelligible species from the sensible species. The intelligible species is totally 'immaterialized' by the action of the agent intellect. Although it alone can be known *directly*, it is that by means of which we *indirectly* know material particulars. The claim is that the intelligible species is really identical with the *form* of the material substance. In that way the objectivity of human knowledge might be preserved. But many Franciscan thinkers held that Aquinas' doctrine generated scepticism because the individuals from which the intelligible species are said ultimately to be derived are not themselves cognizable.[7]   A simpler form of the difficulty even seems present in Aristotle. The individuating matter of a hylemorphically composed substance can only be sensed -- but sensing is not a form of knowing. Both Scotus and Ockham appeal to 'intuitive cognition', i.e. to a mode of cognition of individuals *as existing*, in order to establish a secure foundation for human knowledge.

I contend that we misread Arnauld if we ignore the political dimension to the argument with Malebranche. Malebranche, on the other hand, generally expresses his philosophical goal. It is to secure the object of knowledge, i.e. to establish the reality and independence conditions required for the knowledge we in fact possess -- mathematical knowledge. Descartes had already set out an appropriate theory. Mathematical entities are what they are independently of us. Unlike the things we sense, geometry is what it is regardless of what we may think. For reasons Augustine (and Plato) give, this is the *real world*.

If geometry reveals the real things, how do we 'get' them? If securing the object of knowledge is Malebranche's primary goal, his primary attack is on abstractionism. This is another position he shares with Descartes. The scholastic world was of several minds about whether one could abstract from sensed material individuals anything which could be an object or even a means to an object of knowledge. It was not clear how matter could causally interact with minds, and from the time of Aristotle it had been unclear how, from sensed objects in flux, one could abstract the 'eternal' objects of geometry. Descartes appeals to innate ideas and Malebranche to 'seeing all things in God' because (a) they want to find an ontological 'home' for the objects of cognition, and (b) they know the dismal history of abstractionist 'explanations'.

Descartes employs the notion of something being 'objectively' in the mind in the light of the scholastic tradition. But it is not easy to determine in which scholastic sense it is being used.[8] As already noted, on the Aristotelian-Thomistic model the mind is related to a material substance by a complex 'entity', i.e. an act of perceiving (or whatever) which is itself qualified by the object of that act *as it exists* in the mind. It is usually said that by means of *this* object one cognizes the material substance. This object is the intelligible species, that form which is abstracted from the material substance. But it is probably a mistake to take Descartes' use, at this point, of scholastic terminology too seriously. First, because whatever Descartes' view about material substance is, it is not scholastic in any traditional sense. Indeed, there may really be but one material substance. So the Thomistic parallel breaks down immediately over the notions of 'form' and 'substance'?[9] Second, Descartes is not an abstractionist. In *Meditation* II, for example, Descartes makes it clear that only the pure understanding grasps the essence (extension) of the material world. It does not abstract extension in encounters with material things. Not derived from abstraction, the idea of extension is said to be innate. Finally, we may never *know* if there are *any* material things.

Malebranche and Arnauld argue over the correct reading of Descartes' texts about ideas. Malebranche wants to accord special status to certain of Descartes' ideas, for example of logic and mathematics. He wants to 'dementalize' them; he thinks that if that particular sort of (conceptual) idea is taken to be a mental modification it cannot be about or otherwise represent infinite things - mathematical or theological.[10] Hence Malebranche takes those innate ideas and places them 'in' God. This move is driven by his concern to guarantee the status of the objects of knowledge. He also believes his interpretation is Cartesian in spirit.[11] Arnauld, on the other hand, generally takes Descartes' ideas to be both mental *and* representative. He finds Malebranche's ideas simply extra entities not required either for epistemological or ontological reasons.[12] His basic point, repeated over many pages, appears as Def. 6 in chapter v of *Des vraies et des fausses idées*;[13]

> J'ai dit que je prenais pour la même chose *la perception* et i'*idée*. Il faut néanmoins remarquer que cette chose, quoique unique, a deux rapports: l'un à l'âme qu'elle modifie, l'autre à la chose aperçue, en tant qu'elle est objectivement dans l'âme, et que le mot *perception* marque plus directement le premier rapport, et celui d'*idée* le dernier. Ainsi la *perception* d'un carré marque plus directement mon âme comme apercevant un carré;

> l'*idée* d'un carré marque plus directement le carré, en tant qu'il
> est *objectivement* dans mon esprit...

For the moment, I shall set aside the question of whether Arnauld provides us with the 'direct acquaintance' model Yolton finds, or whether, as Lovejoy and Reid maintain, Arnauld's 'ideas' are themselves 'representive' entities. One of Arnauld's most persistent tactics is to ridicule Malebranche's 'seeing all things in God' doctrine by citing various silly or unpleasant items that are presumably to be 'seen' in God. Beneath the ridicule is a philosophical objection: Malebranche talks about 'seeing all things' but seems to ignore the things we 'know' in the sensed world. However, for Malebranche, there is no knowledge of sensed things, of material particulars. The domain of knowledge is sharply constrained. It is basically a mathematical world. We could have all of the experiences we now have and there be no material world.[14] Were it not for the Biblical revelation we would not know that there is a material world, a claim Berkeley later rejects on the ground that *Genesis* does not speak about material substances. The point, then, is that Malebranche and Arnauld may *appear* to differ radically on whether knowledge extends to existing material individuals.

Malebranche, as noted, takes his doctrine to be fully in accord with Descartes. There is first the strict reading of the role of extension as the essence of the material world in, e.g., the piece of wax example. Second, that extension is grasped by the pure understanding and is grounded on innate ideas, not derived by any sort of abstraction. Third, there is no suggestion in Descartes that we can *know* the piece of wax. Fourth, as the titles of the fifth and sixth *Meditations* show, Descartes is sharply contrasting the essence of things from their existence. It is a contrast Malebranche underscores, although he does not think that Descartes resolves the dream problem in *Meditation* VI. He takes himself to be following the true Descartes by restricting real knowledge to the domain of essence. Malebranche does not deny that we experience encounters with the sensed world. He believes God has given us senses to enable us to survive in that world which, in *Genesis*, He tells us He has created. But we have no means for *knowing* what God has created. As in Descartes, we have no access to God's will, and whatever may exist depends entirely on His will, not on His intellect. That is why we only *know* the essence of the material world. We know the geometrical schema which makes known to us all possible material worlds. The 'in' of Malebranche's notion that things are 'in' Intelligible Extension, is the 'in' of logical containment, as when theorems are said to be 'in' the axioms.[15]

If one looks at Malebranche's picture of an ordinary perceptual situation it contains (a) the knowing mind; (b) an aspect of Intelligible Extension, i.e. some idea 'in' God; (c) a set of sensations. These are modes of the mind; (d) a putative existent material thing. The material thing may, for all we know, be the occasional (but not formal) cause of the sensations. As for the sensations, they are associated with (but again do not formally cause) the Ideas that may 'come to mind'. This association falls under the infinite but unknown laws of conjunction of soul and body. As in Descartes' continual creation system, there are no real connections and no real explanations. We can devise rules of thumb, we can formulate empirical generalizations, but these do not constitute genuine knowledge. Only Ideas are the stuff of knowledge. The moment mere mental modifications enter, we are dealing with 'things' which in some way are mind dependent. And objects of knowledge must be *independent*. Because Arnauld chooses not to see that, he is free to ridicule Malebranche.

Yolton, who wishes to 'de-ontologize' ideas in, e.g. Descartes, Arnauld, and Locke, finds several philosophers (starting with Descartes) who use a sign/thing-signified language metaphor in talking about ideas.[16] Yolton thinks that this helps transform our thinking of causally determined intermediary entities into translucent, as it were, 'semantic' relations. In this way our perceptions can be *about* things without becoming barriers to those very things. I am not so sure. Variations on this 'linguistic' theme are to be found in Stoic theory where they create, as Sextus Empiricus notes, philosophical difficulties.[17] And of course it is to be found in Ockham, Descartes, and especially Louis de la Forge and George Berkeley, as well as in the authors Yolton cites. Minimally, the metaphor is used, as Alquié suggests,[18] to show the arbitrary nature of the relation between sign and thing signified. But it is also used to make a stronger point. The language metaphor is a way of exhibiting that just as the meaning of a word cannot be abstracted from the letters which compose it, so conceptual ideas are not abstracted from either sensory or material data. Thus the question how the mind is 'about' the world, formerly answered by intentional resemblance or identity relations, is now answered by a similarly vacuous equivalent, a semantic relation - a point not lost on Louis de la Forge.

One Cartesian use of the language metaphor has thus to do with exposing the failure of abstractionism as an account of how our ideas or concepts are formed. It constitutes a rejection of a resemblance relation holding between ideas and things. Malebranche's critic, Foucher,[19] argues that resemblance is the only way to explain how ideas can be about things, and he hence seeks to force the collapse of the system, although neither Descartes nor Malebranche claim that the relation is one of resemblance. As just noted, with Cartesian-Malebranchian theories, and more generally with appeals to the language metaphor, the relation is inexplicable. God establishes the relation, which is to say that no human account is available. The difficulty with anti-abstractionism, and with the language metaphor as a weapon against abstractionism, is that a new foundation for ideas or concepts must be found. The Cartesian answer is to find it in the God-imposed structure of the mind or, in the case of Malebranche, in Intelligible Extension.

Descartes argues in *Discours* V that given his system for the understanding of matter (i.e. his mechanical explanations), and given the phenomena that cannot be handled in terms of that physics, a second substance is required - a perfectly reasonable scientific move for that time, as Chomsky has often maintained.[20] But Locke, for example, was not happy with Cartesian dualism. He was particularly unhappy with innate ideas. McCracken suggests,[21] correctly I believe, that Locke attacks Malebranche because he fears that Malebranche was becoming attractive to a number of British philosophers. From the standpoint of an advocate of an empiricist, i.e. abstractionist, theory of knowledge acquisition, Malebranche's doctrine is as dangerous as an innatist theory. Lying behind these various doctrines is the ideological question: the account of human nature we select specifies the extent of human malleability. Locke may ridicule Malebranche in ways that are clearly reminiscent of Arnauld, but there is also a fundamental difference. Neither Arnauld's Cartesianism with respect to certain features of the human mind nor his theological Jansenism would endear him to Locke. And both considerations bear on Arnauld's analysis of Malebranche's so-called 'representative ideas'.

In Malebranche's notion that we 'see all things in God', we actually only 'see' the essence of the material world, Intelligible Extension. We of course *have* sensations, but we do not 'see' them in God. Mental modifications, not being independent of us, are not objects of knowledge. For them, *esse* is *percipi*. To have knowledge of mental phenomena would require an Intelligible Psychology to do for mental substance what Intelligible Extension does for material substance. We have no such thing. We can be aware of smells, tastes, and colours, but we have no conceptual framework in which to place them. Because of our geometrical knowledge we can rigorously specify and explain the difference between a circle and a square. Nothing similar can be done to exhibit the essential natures of, e.g., one colour and another. Malebranche thus offers us a radical asymmetry between our knowledge of material and mental substance in addition to that between essence and existence. Malebranche criticises the 'other' Cartesians who take a different tack with respect to the essence of mental substance. Louis de la Forge does produce a Cartesian style psychology but he primarily offers us useful metaphors and illuminating analogues rather than an explanatory theory which lays bare the essence of the human mind.

Arnauld, on the other hand, strives to do just that. He opens up a very different set of possibilities. His *Port Royal Grammar* constitutes a systematic effort to produce - in the Cartesian spirit - the

40

principles of the essence of the human mind. The insight behind his Cartesian dream is simplicity itself. The basic idea can be put in this ratio: grammar is to mind as geometry is to matter. Arnauld and Port Royal may have failed in the execution of this insight. In the end they were unable to produce that Universal Grammar which would characterize the essence of the human mind. Having tried to produce a theoretical, and not merely descriptive account of the mind, Arnauld was entitled to be 'philosophically' displeased, as it were, to find Malebranche excluding minds from the scope of human knowledge. Universal Grammar is not, however, a theme discussed in his extended criticism of Malebranche. One may wish that Arnauld's theory of mind might help provide at least a partially philosophical explanation from Arnauld's harping on the 'ridiculous' idea that for Malebranche, we are first said to see all things in God and then we discover that we do not see mental phenomena or its essence, but I fear the truth of the matter lies elsewhere.

Although my sympathies are with Lovejoy's interpretation of representative ideas, I shall not recapitulate the debate. Instead, I now propose briefly to look at Lennon's 'direct realist' approach to Arnauld.[22] Lennon argues that we can distinguish the 'intentionality' of ideas from the question of direct realism. Roughly speaking, the intentionality issue ("how is it that the mind is aware of this object rather than that" [794]) is answered by saying that "the mind is qualitatively tied to its object" [795], as in those scholastic theories which claim that there is an identity between the form in the mind (the intelligible species) and the form in the material substance. As I note above, the identity claim proved difficult to sustain in the face of the attacks on abstractionism. Indeed, the attack on this type of intentionality is already present in the Greek sceptics. The intentional 'likeness' or 'identity' claim presupposes that one can intelligibly introduce a binary relation in contexts where *in principle* one has access only to *one* term. The Cartesian notion of things which are objectively in the mind is the Cartesian version of intentionality, except that the 'form in the mind' is not abstracted from the putative material substance and does not stand in a relation of likeness to it. The *possible* material thing is 'made known' by these conceptual entities, as Descartes explains at the outset of *Meditation* VI.

According to Lennon, "a direct or presentationalist view has it that we directly perceive physical objects" [795]. The representationalist argues against this on the basis of perceptual error, etc., and hence that we must include a mental entity which we directly perceive as opposed to the physical object we are then said to perceive indirectly. Lennon holds that all parties to the dispute begin with some sort of pre-philosophical common-sensical awareness of physical objects and secondly, that the representationalist move undercuts the 'intentionality' principle. But the first point is by definition philosophically and scientifically uninteresting and the second begs the question. In any event, Lennon believes that Arnauld advances a direct realist account of perception - one which is philosophically fraught with fewer difficulties than Malebranche's doctrine. Lennon also calls our attention to a very important feature of Arnauld's story: according to Arnauld, 'the object of nonveridical awareness is a possible object.[23]'

What are we to make of this notion that our perception-ideas, already 'representative', are 'about' possible objects? I have presented a brief sketch of what I think of as Arnauld's theory of the essence of the human mind in terms of grammar. I suggested that this can be seen in both dualist and anti-abstractionist terms despite what may seem like a Thomist theory of intentionality (based in large part on Arnauld's talk about how things are 'objectively' in the mind). When we turn to his theory of mind we find a rationalist model, one with a theory of grammar which will do for mind what geometry does for body. And now we find him talking about perceiving *possible* objects. Although this makes the direct realist interpretation incoherent, I am especially interested in the traditional Cartesianism which now stands revealed in his theory of possible objects. Not surprisingly, the *Port Royal Logic* opens with a fierce attack on the abstractionist/empiricist thesis that there is nothing in the intellect which is not first in the senses.[24]

In the titles of the fifth *Meditation*, as I have mentioned, Descartes speaks of the *essence* of material things and in the sixth, of their *existence*. Having drawn a sharp distinction between essence and existence, and having constrained the domain of clear and distinct to *essence*, existent things (with the exceptions of oneself and God), cannot - strictly speaking - be known.[25] That is, since we can only be said to know what is clear and distinct, material things (as well as sensations), not being perceived with clarity *and* distinctness, cannot be known. Malebranche, like Hobbes, did not think Descartes' apparent 'solution' to the dream problem at the end of *Meditation* VI brought the world of sensed objects into the domain of knowledge. Certainly the suggestion in *Meditations* V and VI is that essentially cognized material things are only possible objects. Whether they exist depends on God's will. All that Descartes will grant is that:

> At least I now know that [material things] are capable of existing, in so far as they are the subject-matter of pure mathematics, since I perceive them clearly and distinctly. For there is no doubt that God is capable of creating everything that I am capable of perceiving in this manner...[26]

The thesis that the object of perception is a possible object can thus be ascribed to Descartes. Indeed, in *VFI* (as commentators have noted) Arnauld occasionally even talks about our having to *reason* our way from ideas to things.[27] Even though he believes it is certain that there are things outside us, such things are not given directly. Moreover, Arnauld allows that God may have arranged corporeal movements in the senses as occasional causes for our perceptions.[28]

Monte Cook has sought to unravel the complexities of the debate over representative ideas. He suggests that Arnauld tends to undercut his own presentationalist account by trying to remain a proper Cartesian, although he too grants that what counts as a Cartesian object of knowledge is complicated. My view is that Malebranche is correct in his interpretation of Descartes, i.e. sensations are not objects of knowledge although reflections upon such perceptions support the truth of the *cogito*. By separating out Descartes' conceptual ideas, and making clear that they are not mental modifications in the sense that sensations are, Malebranche wants Ideas which are ontologically independent of us and which are *public*.[29]

Yolton, Cook and Lennon find a strand of presentational realism in Arnauld. Cook speaks of Arnauld's 'act theory of ideas'. Is this the Mental Language act theory found already in Ockham? If so, the difficulties are evident. Ockham is committed to intuitive cognition of individuals. That means that his act theory of ideas is tied by an 'aboutness' relation to an individual whose *existence* is *known* with certainty. Whatever Cartesians (such as Arnauld) do, they do not attempt to base knowledge on such intuitively cognized building blocks.

I have throughout focused on the question of anti-abstractionism because I think it is an essential feature of Cartesianism. However, the problem of how minds can know material things already arises in the middle ages when theologians try to explain how pure minds, i.e. angels, can have abstractive knowledge when they lack bodily sense organs. It forced them to consider non-abstractive theories of concept acquisition. Desmond Connell has shown how important Suarez' *Treatise on the angels* was to Malebranche.[30] Once empiricist, i.e. abstractionist, accounts of concept acquisition are rejected, once one takes seriously the sorts of dualism already fully present in discussions of angelic vs. human knowledge, then innateness or 'seeing all things in God' become the only philosophically viable answers.

I have said that the fundamental question for Malebranche and, as he sees it, for Descartes, is to secure an object of knowledge which is totally independent of us. That is why he will not countenance perceptions as representative in the Arnauld style. And why he repeatedly tries to show that even in Descartes, that which is 'objectively' in the mind is to be distinguished from the sort of mental activity it is associated with. Arnauld's perception-ideas may have some sort of 'constituent' which qualifies the mental act involved, but he claims that these ideas are nevertheless ontological simples. Unlike Malebranche, he does not accept the principle that what is

43

distinguishable is separable - at least when it is applied to ideas. The problem with Arnauld's side of this controversy is that he is personally enraged by Malebranche's theological views. His goal is not philosophical - it is to inflict maximum damage on Malebranche's philosophical reputation so that his theological opinions will not be taken seriously. In that Arnauld is successful. He has no other stake in the polemic over representative ideas, although I have tried to give him one, namely the radical theory he advances elsewhere that grammar can reveal the essence of the mind. That is not only a major contribution to Cartesian-style theorizing about the mind, it is Arnauld's most important contribution to philosophy. Had his polemical concerns been primarily philosophical one might have expected that he would have directly confronted Malebranche on this genuinely fundamental point of disagreement between them. He does no such thing.

In summary, there are problems with treating Arnauld as a proponent of any form of direct or presentational realism. If one ignores his strong attack on the abstractionist/empiricist account of concept acquisition in the *Logic* and then proceeds to attribute to him the view that our concepts are formed by abstraction from sensed individuals, then one must find a way for Arnauld to do what Aquinas is unable to do, namely to explain how we can have direct *cognitive* acquaintance of entities whose sensed (i.e. material) individuality cannot be abstracted into the conceptual domain. Secondly, if one attributes to Arnauld the view that what is objectively-in-the-mind is there via abstraction and that it stands in a relation of identity or resemblance to existent material individuals, then that position is incompatible with several of the Cartesian elements in his philosophy, e.g. his innatism. Third, if one takes presentative ('direct') realism to include (as one should) *intuitive* cognition of existent individuals à la Scotus and Ockham, that thesis is incompatible with Arnauld's counting possible objects as the objects of perception. Furious at Malebranche's dissent from Jansenism, Arnauld's attack is intended to destroy him. No coherent philosophical position supports his attack. No wonder Laird and Lovejoy argued about Arnauld's true position. But there is no 'true position'.

Malebranche's philosophical goal is straightforward. He seeks to establish, in a clearer form than that found in Descartes, a proper object of knowledge, one which is both non-subjective and ontologically independent. So we are left to speculate on why the philosophical tradition from Locke onwards has tended to side with Arnauld. I suggest it may be because we prefer empiricist accounts of human nature, accounts within which humans are seen as malleable objects suitable for control, rather than innately structured autonomous beings as in the Cartesian account.[31] One may wish to try to force Arnauld into an empiricist mold, or like Locke, merely use the

Arnauld/Malebranche polemics as an occasion for attacking rationalism, or both. As is often the case with the 'construction' of the history of philosophy, the point is ideological.

Notes

1. I am particularly indebted to Elly van Gelderen for commenting on earlier drafts of this paper. I wish also to thank Professor S. C. Brown for a variety of useful editorial suggestions.

2. A few of the contributors to this discussion are: Monte Cook, "Arnauld's alleged representationalism", *Journal of the History of Philosophy*, XII (1974), 53-62; G. Dawes Hicks, "Sense perception and thought", *Proc. Arist. Soc.* NS, VI (1905-06), 271-346, esp. 275 f; John Laird, *A study of realism*, (Cambridge: UP, 1920), and his "The 'legend' of Arnauld's realism", *Mind*, XXXIII (1924), 176-9; Thomas M. Lennon, "Philosophical commentary", in Nicolas Malebranche, *The search after truth*, transl. Thomas M. Lennon and Paul J. Olscamp, (Columbus: Ohio State UP, 1980); Arthur O. Lovejoy, "'Representative ideas' in Malebranche and Arnauld", *Mind*, XXXII (1923), 449-61 and his "Reply to Professor Laird", *Mind*, XXXIII (1924), 180-1; Steven M. Nadler, "Reid, Arnauld and the objects of perception", *History of Philosophy Quarterly*, III (1986), 165-73; Daisie Radner, "Representationalism in Arnauld's act theory of perception", *Journal of the History of Philosophy*, XIV (1976), 96-8; Thomas Reid, Essay II, ch. xiii, *Essays on the intellectual powers of man*, in *Philosophical works*, notes by Sir Wm Hamilton, intro, by Harry M. Bracken, 2 vols. (Hildesheim: Olms, 1967); Ian Tipton, "'Ideas' in Berkeley and Arnauld", *History of European Ideas*, VII (1986), 575-84; John W. Yolton, *Perceptual Acquaintance from Descartes to Reid* (Minneapolis: U of MnP, 1984). Since preparing this paper I have come upon Steven M. Nadler, *Arnauld and the Cartesian philosophy of ideas*, (Manchester: UP, 1989), an extended and important discussion of these themes from a 'direct realist' vantage point.

3. All my references to Malebranche are to *Oeuvres complètes de Malebranche*, 20 vols., general editor, André Robinet, (Paris: Vrin, 1958 f.). The *Traité de la nature et de la grâce* is in *OCM* vol. V (1958), ed. Ginette Dreyfus. See her edition of *TNG* (Paris: Vrin, 1958). Her "Introduction philosophique", 3, is devoted to "La polémique avec Arnauld". she writes: "L'attaque contre le *Traité de la nature et de la grâce* s'engage indirectment, par une critique de la théorie des idées". (p. 53). The machinations of Arnauld and his friends are said to have prompted Rome to put the *TNG* on the Index. Cf. Francisque Bouiller, *Histoire de la philosophie cartésienne*, 3rd. ed. (Paris: Delagrave, 1868), II, 24.

4. "La Traité de la Nature & de la Grace, ayant fait connoître à Messieurs de Port-Royal, que l'Auteur de la *Recherche de la Verité* n'étoit point Janseniste, comme ils l'avoient crû, n'eut pas le bonheur de leur plaire. C'est pourquoi ils donnerent commission à M. Arnauld de la réfuter..." Pierre Bayle, *Oeuvres diverses* (Den Haag: Husson et al., 1727), I, 25a. (*NRL*, Avril 1684, art II).

5. Yolton, *Perceptual acquaintance*, p. 6.

6. *PA*, p. 7. Yolton recognizes that Aristotle seems to say that we sense individuals but know universals and that in Aquinas this contrast is more complex.

7. Cf. Sebastian Day, *Intuitive cognition: a key to the significance of the later scholastics*. (St. Bonaventure: Franciscan Institute, 1947).

8. Perhaps it is Scotistic. See Calvin Normore, "Meaning and objective being: Descartes and his sources", in *Essays on Descartes' Meditations*, ed. A. O. Rorty. (Berkeley: University California Press, 1986), 223-41, esp. p. III f., and Helen S. Lang, "Bodies and angels: the occupants of place for Aristotle and Duns Scotus", *Viator*, XIV (1983), 245-66. On Suarez see, e.g. Norman J. Wells, "Suarez on the eternal truths", *Modern Schoolman*, LVIII (1981), 73-104; 159-74 and his "Objective reality of ideas in Descartes, Caterus, and Suárez", *Journal of the History of Philosophy*, XXVIII (1990), 33-61. See also the work of T. J. Cronin.

9. Descartes' difficulties are well known, but cf. J. R. Armogathe, *Theologia cartesiana*, (Den Haag: Nijhoff, 1977).

10. Malebranche and Arnauld discuss, e.g. *Meditation III*. At *Meditation V*, [*AT* VII, 64] Descartes speaks of certain ideas as being eternal and immutable. Malebranche holds that given these properties, such ideas could not be modifications of our minds.

11. Cf. *OCM*, VI-VII, 215 f.

12. Arnauld's argument sometimes appears to be a re-run of Aristotle's attack on Plato's Ideas. Cf. *VFI*, end of chapter xiv, in *Oeuvres de Messire Antoine Arnauld...* Reprint of the 1775 f. ed. (Brussels: Culture & Civilisation, 1967), XXXVIII, 258.

13. Def. 6, *OAA*, XXXVIII, 198.

14. E.g., *Entretiens sur la métaphysique...*VI, viii; *OCM*, XII-XIII, 142.

15.   I remain convinced by the analyses of Paul Schrecker, "Le parallélisme théologico-mathématique chez Malebranche", *Revue philosophique*, XXXV (1938), 215-52; and Léon Brunschvicg, *Les étapes de la philosophie mathématique*, 3rd. ed. (Paris: PUF, 1947). See also Gustav Bergmann, "Some remarks on the philosophy of Malebranche", in his *Meaning and existence*, (Madison University of Wisconsin Pr., 1960), 189-204, and my "Some problems of substance among the Cartesians", *American philosophical quarterly*, I (1964), 129-37.

16.   This is discussed at some length in my *Berkeley* (London: Macmillan, 1974), ch. xi.

17.   E.g., *Adv. Math.* viii, 153-5. For a range of references to the texts of Sextus Empiricus cf. Benson Mates, *Stoic logic*, (Berkeley: University of California Press, 1961), pp. 13 f.

18.   *Descartes: oeuvres philosophiques*, ed. F. Alquié, 3 vols. (Paris: Garnier Frères, 1963) I, 316n.

19.   Cf. Richard A. Watson, *Breakdown of Cartesian metaphysics*, (Atlantic Highlands, NJ: Humanities Press, 1987).

20.   Most recently in his *Language and problems of knowledge: the Manaua lectures.* (Cambridge: MIT Press, 1988) esp. 136-52.

21.   Charles J. McCracken, *Malebranche and British philosophy*, (Oxford: Clarendon Press, 1983), p. 119.

22.   In his "Philosophical Commentary" to his Malebranche, *Search*, referred to above in my note 2.

23.   *Ibid.*, p. 803, citing Arnauld, OAA , XXXVIII, 221.

24.   Cf. *Port Royal Logic*, Pt. I, ch. i..

25.   Malebranche, *OCM*, e.g. VI-VII, 182 f.

26.   *The philosophical writings of Descartes*, transl. John Cottingham, Robert Stoothoff, and Dugald Murdoch. 2 vols. (Cambridge: UP., 1984), II, 50 [*AT* VII, 71].

27.   *VFI*, ch. V, p. 9. *OAA*, XXXVIII, 199.

28.   *VFI*, chs. VI and VII. *OAA*, XXXVIII, 209, 212.

29.   E.g., *OCM*, VIII-IX, 1000.

30.   Desmond Connell, *The vision in God: Malebranche's scholastic sources*.
       (Leuven: Éditions Nauwelaerts, 1967).

31.   I discuss this in my *Mind and language: essays on Descartes and Chomsky*.
       (Dordrecht: FORIS, 1984), esp. ch. i.

5   Divine and Human Will in the Philosophy of Malebranche

PATRICK RILEY

The notion of 'will' is central in Malebranche's conception of God and of man: unless God has a will (*en général*) he cannot have a 'general will' (*en particulier*) to rule the universe through simple, constant, uniform 'Cartesian' natural laws which he creates (avoiding all *ad hoc* 'particular wills' and miraculous interventions in nature)[1]; unless man has a will he cannot freely and meritoriously determine himself to embrace *le bien général*, 'order', and 'relations of perfection', while shunning deceptive *biens particuliers*[2] Both God and man must will the general and flee the particular in Malebranche: God does so 'naturally' (as it were), since *généralité* is 'worthy' of him; men must strive to do so, with the help of Christ-distributed grace. What this means is that 'will' is nearly as important to Malebranche as to more celebrated voluntarists such as Augustine or Kant (with their notions of *bona voluntas* and 'good will'); and though Malebranche's occasionalism (which deprives finite creatures of true causality) is problematical for human free will, real self-determination, it remains true that *malebranchisme* contains an important voluntarist strand. God simply has *a volonté générale*, and men ought to strive to have one – as Malebranche's great *Traité de la nature et de la grâce* (1680) makes clear.

It should be remembered that Malebranche developed his notion of divine 'general will,' in the first instance, as an interpretation of a famous saying of St. Paul's: 'God wills that all men be saved.' In the sixteenth 'Eclaircissement' of *De la recherche de la vérité*, which Malebranche appended to the third edition in 1678, he argues that, 'while God wills to save us all,' the fact that he operates through 'the simplest means' – through uniform *volontés générales*, not through a multiplicity of *volontés particulières* – means that some will *not* be saved. (Here 'general will' is associated with Cartesian constancy, uniformity and economy.) This was to be elaborated in *Nature et grâce*; but the sixteenth 'Eclaircissement' of the *Recherche* contains a defect that was not carried over into the *Traité* and that doubtless led to the final abandoning of this 'Eclaircissement'. Urging again that God acts 'always by the simplest means...in virtue of general wills,' Malebranche observes that the Ten Commandments were written by the ancient Jews over their doorways and argues that this 'spared' God a particular will, 'if one can speak in this way, to inspire these [righteous] thoughts in them.'[3] Obviously, a perfect being does not need to be 'spared' anything, even a *volonté particulière*, since the notion of 'need' is meaningless for such a being. This is best pointed out, nearly a hundred years later, in the theological *Briefwechsel* between Julie de Wolmar and St. Preux that Rousseau inserts in book 6 of *La Nouvelle Héloïse*, in which Julie mockingly points out to the Malebranchian St. Preux that only human beings need economy, that God does not need man to 'abridge his work' for him by following ready-made general rules. (St. Preux responds that 'it is worthy of his wisdom to prefer the simplest means.'[4]) A similar thought must have crossed Malebranche's mind – even in the sixteenth 'Eclaircissement' he says, 'if one can speak in this way' – and in *Nature et grâce*, the simplicity and generality of God's action is grounded, not in any need for economy or sparing divine labor, but in the notion that simplicity and generality of willing best *express* divine perfection.[5]

In the 'Premier Eclaircissement' of the *Traité de la nature et de la grâce*, one sees at once that Malebranche is not going to treat divine *volonté générale* as something confined to theology, to questions of grace and merit; one sees that he intends to treat general will as something that is manifested in *all* of God's operations – as much in the realm of nature as in that of grace. Malebranche argues that 'God acts by *volontés générales* when he acts as a consequence of general laws which he has established.' Nature, he adds, 'is nothing but the general laws which God has established in order to construct or to preserve his work by the simplest means, by an action [that is] always uniform, constant, perfectly worthy of an infinite wisdom and of a universal cause.[6]   God, on this view, does not act by *volontés particulières*, by lawless ad hoc volitions, as do 'limited intelligences' whose thought is not 'infinite.'[7]   Thus, for Malebranche, 'to establish general laws, and to choose the simplest ones which are at the same time the most fruitful, is a way of acting worthy of him whose wisdom has no limits.' On the other hand, 'to act by *volontés particulières* shows a limited intelligence which cannot judge the consequences or the effects of less fruitful causes.'[8]

Even at this point, Malebranche's argument, though mainly a theological one, contains some points that could be read 'legally': the general will manifests itself in general laws that are 'fruitful' and 'worthy' of infinite wisdom, whereas particular will is 'limited', comparatively unintelligent,   and lawless.   Indeed Malebranche himself occasionally 'politicizes' his argument, particularly in his effort to *justify* God's acting (exclusively) through *volontés générales*. If 'rain falls on certain lands, and if the sun roasts others...if a child comes into the world with a malformed and useless head...this is not at all because God wanted to produce those effects by *volontés particulières*; it is because he has established [general] laws for the communication of motion, whose effects are necessary consequences.' Thus, according to Malebranche, 'one cannot say that God acts through caprice or ignorance' in permitting malformed children to be born or unripe fruit to fall. 'He has not established the laws of the communication of motion for the purpose of producing monsters, or of making fruits fall before their maturity'; he has willed these laws 'because of their fruitfulness, and not because of their sterility.'[9]   Those who claim that God *ought*, through special, ad hoc *volontés particulières*, to suspend natural laws if their operation will harm the virtuous or the innocent, or that he ought to confer grace only on those who will actually be saved by it, fail to understand that it is not worthy of an infinitely wise being to abandon general rules in order to find a suppositious perfect fit between the particular case of each finite being and a *volonté particulière* suited to that case alone.[10]

By this point, evidently, the theological notion of *volonté générale* is becoming 'legalized.'   *Volonté générale* originally manifested itself in general laws that were wise and fruitful; now that will, expressed in those laws, is *just* as well, and it is quite wrong to say that God ought to contrive a *volonté particulière* suited to each case, even though the generaility of his will and of his laws will mean that grace will occasionally fall on a hardened heart incapable of receiving it.[11]   God, Malebranche urges, loves his wisdom more than he loves mankind ('c'est que Dieu aime davantage sa sagesse que son ouvrage')[12], and his wisdom is expressed in general laws, the operation of which may have consequences (monstrous children, unripened fruit) that are not *themselves* willed and that cannot therefore give rise to charges of divine caprice or ignorance.

If Malebranche, in pleading the 'cause' of God (to use Leibniz's phrase),[13] views divine *volonté générale* as issuing in wise and just laws, the *Traité de la nature et de la grâce* is further (and quite explicitly) politicized by an analogy that Malebranche himself draws between a well-governed earthly kingdom and a well-governed Creation. He begins with an argument about enlightened and unenlightened will: 'The more enlightened an agent is, the more extensive are his *volontés*. A very limited mind undertakes new schemes at every moment; and when he wants to execute one of them, he uses several means, of which some are always useless.' But a 'broad and penetrating mind,' he goes on, 'compares and weighs all things: he never forms plans except with the knowledge that he has the means to execute them.'[14] Malebranche then moves to his political analogy: 'A great number of laws in a state'–presumably a mere concatenation of many *volontés particulières*–' often shows little penetration and breadth of mind in those who have established them: it is often the mere experience of need, rather than wise foresight, which has ordained them' God *qua* legislator has none of these defects, Malebranche claims: 'He need not multiply his *volontés*, which are the executive laws of his plans, any further than necessity obliges.' He must act through *volontés générales* 'and thus establish a constant and regulated order' by 'the simplest means.' Those who want God to act, not through 'les loix ou les volontés générales,' but through *volontés particulières*, simply 'imagine that God at every moment is performing miracles in their favor.' This partisanship for the particular, Malebranche says, 'flatters the self-love which relates everything to itself,' and 'accommodates itself quite well' to ignorance![5]

Malebranche certainly believed that those who imagine a God thick with *volontés particulières* will use that alleged divine particularism to rationalize their own failure to embrace general principles. Indeed, he appeals to the notion of *particularisme* in attempting to explain the lamentable diversity of the world's moral opinions and practices. In the *Traité de morale* (1684) Malebranche argues that although 'universal reason is always the same' and 'order is immutable,' 'morality changes according to countries and according to the times.' Germans think it virtuous to drink to excess; European nobles think it 'generous' to fight duels in defense of their honor. Such people 'even imagine that God approves their conduct,' that, in the case of an aristocratic duel, he 'presides at the judgement and…awards the palm to him who is right.' Of course, one can only imagine this if one thinks that God acts by *volontés particulières*. And if even he is thought to operate particularly, why should not men as well? The man who imputes particular wills to God by 'letting himself be led by

imagination, his enemy,' will also have his own '*morale particulière,
his own devotion, his favorite virtue.*' What is essential is that one
abandon *particularisme*, whether as something ascribed to God or as
something merely derived from human 'inclinations' and 'humors.' It
is 'immutable order' that must serve as our 'inviolable and natural law,'
and 'imagination' that must be suppressed. For order is general, while
imagination is all too particular.[16]

So wise, constant, and just are God's *volontés générales*, in
Malebranche's view, that it is a moral wrong on man's part not to
accept and respect these general wills and to make them the measure of
human conduct. In one of his numerous defenses of *Nature et grâce*,
Malebranche argues that 'if God did not act in consequence of general
laws which he has established, no one would ever make any effort.
Instead of descending a staircase step by step, one would rather throw
himself out of the windows, trusting himself to God.' Why would it be
sin as well as folly to hurl oneself from a window? 'It would be sin,'
Malebranche answers, 'because it would be tempting God: it would be
claiming to obligate him to act in a manner unworthy of him, or
through *volonté particulières*'; it would amount to telling God 'that his
work is going to perish, if he himself does not trouble the simplicity of
his ways.' In addition to sin, of course, hurling oneself would be folly,
for one must be mad to imagine that 'God must regulate his action by
our particular needs, and groundlessly change, out of love for us, the
uniformity of his conduct.'[17]

For Malebranche's orthodox and conservative critics – most
notably Bossuet, whose anti-Malebranchism will be treated shortly –
perhaps the most distressing aspect of Malebranche's theory of divine
volonté générale was the much-diminished weight and value given to
literally read Scripture. In *Nature et grâce* Malebranche urges that
'those who claim that God has particular plans and wills for all the
particular effects which are produced in consequence of general laws'
ordinarily rely not on philosophy but on the authority of Scripture to
'shore up' their 'feeling.' (The verb and noun are sufficiently
revealing.) But, Malebranche argues, 'since Scripture was made for
everybody, for the simple as well as for the learned, it is full of
anthropologies.' Scripture, continues Malebranche, endows God with
'a body, a throne, a chariot, a retinue, the passions of joy, of sadness,
of anger, of remorse, and the other movements of the soul'; it even
goes beyond this and attributes to him 'ordinary human ways of acting,
in order to speak to the simple in a more sensible way.' St. Paul, in
order to accommodate himself to everyone, speaks of sanctification
and predestination 'as if God acted ceaselessly' through *volonté
particulières* to produce those particular effects; even Christ himself
'speaks of his father as if he applied himself, through comparable
volontés, to clothe the lilies of the field and to preserve the least hair
on his disciples' heads.' Despite all these 'anthropologies' and 'as ifs,'

imagination, his enemy,' will also have his own *'morale particulière*, his own devotion, his favorite virtue.' What is essential is that one abandon *particularisme*, whether as something ascribed to God or as something merely derived from human 'inclinations' and 'humors.' It is 'immutable order' that must serve as our 'inviolable and natural law,' and 'imagination' that must be suppressed. For order is general, while imagination is all too particular.[16]

So wise, constant, and just are God's *volontés générales*, in Malebranche's view, that it is a moral wrong on man's part not to accept and respect these general wills and to make them the measure of human conduct. In one of his numerous defenses of *Nature et grâce*, Malebranche argues that 'if God did not act in consequence of general laws which he has established, no one would ever make any effort. Instead of descending a staircase step by step, one would rather throw himself out of the windows, trusting himself to God.' Why would it be sin as well as folly to hurl oneself from a window? 'It would be sin,' Malebranche answers, 'because it would be tempting God: it would be claiming to obligate him to act in a manner unworthy of him, or through *volonté particulières*'; it would amount to telling God 'that his work is going to perish, if he himself does not trouble the simplicity of his ways.' In addition to sin, of course, hurling oneself would be folly, for one must be mad to imagine that 'God must regulate his action by our particular needs, and groundlessly change, out of love for us, the uniformity of his conduct.'[17]

III

For Malebranche's orthodox and conservative critics – most notably Bossuet, whose anti-Malebranchism will be treated shortly – perhaps the most distressing aspect of Malebranche's theory of divine *volonté générale* was the much-diminished weight and value given to literally read Scripture. In *Nature et grâce* Malebranche urges that 'those who claim that God has particular plans and wills for all the particular effects which are produced in consequence of general laws' ordinarily rely not on philosophy but on the authority of Scripture to 'shore up' their 'feeling.' (The verb and noun are sufficiently revealing.) But, Malebranche argues, 'since Scripture was made for everybody, for the simple as well as for the learned, it is full of *anthropologies*.' Scripture, continues Malebranche, endows God with 'a body, a throne, a chariot, a retinue, the passions of joy, of sadness, of anger, of remorse, and the other movements of the soul'; it even goes beyond this and attributes to him 'ordinary human ways of acting, in order to speak to the simple in a more sensible way.' St. Paul, in order to accommodate himself to everyone, speaks of sanctification and predestination 'as if God acted ceaselessly' through *volonté particulières* to produce those particular effects; even Christ himself 'speaks of his father as if he applied himself, through comparable *volontés*, to clothe the lilies of the field and to preserve the least hair on his disciples' heads.' Despite all these 'anthropologies' and 'as ifs,' our weakness, sometimes represents God as a man, and often has him act as men act.[24] Here, as in the main text of *Nature et grâce*, the key notion is weakness, and any notion of divine *volonté particulière* simply accommodates that *foiblesse*. This is why Malebranche can maintain – this time in the "Troisième Eclaircissement" of 1683 – that 'there are ways of acting [that are] simple, fruitful, general, uniform and constant,' and that manifest 'wisdom, goodness, steadiness [and] immutability in those who use them.' On the other hand, there are also ways that are 'complex, sterile, particular, lawless and inconstant,' and that reveal 'lack of intelligence, malignity, unsteadiness [and] levity in those who use them.'[25] Thus, a very effective heap of execrations is mounded around any *volonté particulière*, which turns out to be complex, sterile, lawless, inconstant, unintelligent, malignant, and frivolous.

Indeed, for Malebranche it is precisely *volonté particulière*, and not *volonté générale*, that 'ruins' Providence. In his *Réponse à une dissertation de M. Arnauld contre un élaircissement de la nature et de la grâce* (1685), he argues that, if Arnauld's insistence on miracles and constant divine *volontés particulières* does not 'overturn' Providence, it at least 'degrades it, humanizes it, and makes it either blind, or perverse.'

> Is there wisdom in creating monsters by *volontés particulières*? In making crops grow by rainfall, in order to ravage them by hail? In giving to men a thousand impulses of grace which misfortunes render useless? In making rain fall equally on sand and on cultivated ground? But all this is nothing. Is there wisdom and gooodness in making impious princes reign, in suffering so great a number of heresies, in letting so many nations perish? Let M. Arnauld raise his head and discover all the evils which happen in the world, and let him justify Providence, on the supposition that God acts and must act through *volontés particulières*.[26]

It is Malebranche's view, in fact, that the classical 'theodicy problems' of reconciling a morally and physically imperfect world with God's 'power,' 'goodness,' and 'wisdom' can *only* be solved by insisting that God wills generally. Malebranche states these problems starkly in *Nature et grâce*.

> Holy Scripture teaches us on [the] one hand that God wills that all men be saved, and that they come to a knowledge of the truth; and on the other, that he does everything that he wills: and nonetheless faith is not given to everyone; and the number of those that perish is much greater than that of the predestined. How can one reconcile this with his power?

God foresaw from all eternity [both] original sin, and the infinite number of persons that this sin would sweep into Hell. Nonetheless he created the first man in a condition from which he knew he would fall; he even established between this man and his posterity relations which would communicate his sin to them, and render them all worthy of his aversion and his wrath. How can one reconcile this with his goodness?

God frequently diffuses graces, without having the effect for which his goodness obliges us to blieve that he gives them. He increases piety in persons almost to the end of their life; and sin dominates them at death, and throws them into Hell. He makes the rain of grace fall on hardened hearts, as well as on prepared grounds: men resist it, and make it useless for their salvation. In a word, God undoes and re-does without cease: it seems that he wills, and no longer wills. How can one reconcile this with his wisdom?[27]

According to Malebranche, these 'great difficulties' are cleared up by the generality and simplicity of divine will. Its possession of these characteristics also explains how a being who loves order can permit disorder. 'God loves men, he wills to save them all,' Malebranche asserts, 'for order is his law.' Nonetheless, God 'does not will to *do* what is necessary in order that all [men] know him and love him infallibly,' and this is simply because 'order does not permit that he have practical *volontés* proper to the execution of this design...He must not disturb the simplicity of his ways.'[28] Or, as Malebranche puts it in his *Réponse* to Arnauld's *Réflexions on Nature et grâce*,

The greater number of men are damned, and [yet] God wills to save them all...Whence comes it, then, that sinners die in their sin? Is it better to maintain that God does *not* will to save them all, simply because it pleases him to act in that way, than to seek the general reason for it in what he owes to himself, to his wisdom, and to his other attributes? Is it not clear, or at least is it not a feeling in conformity with piety, that one must throw these unhappy effects back onto simplicity – in one word onto the divinity of his ways?[29]

In his final work, published in the year of his death (1715), Malebranche reformulated this argument in an even stronger way – a way that Leibniz, among others, found excessive.

Infinity in all sorts of perfections is an attribute of the divinity, indeed his essential attribute, that which encloses all the others. Now between the finite and the infinite, the distance is infinite; the relation is nothing. The most excellent of creatures, compared to the divinity, is nothing; and God counts it as nothing in relation to himself...It seems to me evident, that God conducts himself according to what he is, in remaining immobile, [even while] seeing the demon tempt, and man succumb to the temptation...His immobility bears the character of his infinity...If God, in order to stop the Fall of Adam, had interrupted the ordinary course of his *providence générale*, that conduct would have expressed the false judgment that God had counted the worship that Adam rendered him as something, with respect to his infinite majesty. Now God must never trouble the simplicity of his ways, nor interrupt the wise, constant and majestic course of his ordinary providence, by a particular and miraculous providence...God is infinitely wise, infinitely just, infinitely good, and he does men all the good he can – not absolutely, but acting according to what he is...[30]

After this, Malebranche's insistence that, nonetheless, 'God sincerely wills to save all men' rings a little hollow. It is no wonder that Leibniz, for all his general agreement with Malebranche, should complain that 'I do not know whether one should have recourse to the expedient [of saying] that God, by remaining immobile during the Fall of man...marks [in that way] that the most excellent creatures are nothing in relation to him.' For Leibniz, that way of putting the matter can be abused, and can even lead to 'the despotism of the supralapsarians.'[31] Perhaps the 'immobility' passage was the one that the Jesuit Rodolphe Du Tertre had in mind when he published a three-volume attack of Malebranche even as the Oratorian lay on his deathbed; in the final volume of his *Réfutation d'un nouveau système de métaphysique proposé par la Père Malebranche*, Du Tertre argues that

according to our author [Malebranche], God wills to save all men in this sense, that the ways...that he was indispensably obliged to follow in the execution of his work, will cause to enter into the future Church the most men that simplicity and generality will permit. [God] wills that all men be saved in this sense, that if there could be some other order of grace, equally worthy of him and more useful to men...he would have chosen it, or rather he would have been necessitated by his wisdom to choose it, in order not to contradict his attributes. There once again one sees what Father M[alebranche] calls God's true will that all men be saved – though at the same time he assures us that God cannot save more than he does save, without performing miracles that immutable order, which is his necessary law, does not permit him to perform...

This means that the new theologican judges it suitable, for good reasons, to give the name 'true and sincere will' to a chimerical *velléité* which it pleases him to imagine in God with respect to the salvation of men; such that, according to [Malebranche's] dictionary, to say that God truly wills that all men be saved is really to say that God would will this, if it could be, though it cannot be: that he would will it, supposing an impossible hypothesis, which would be that there is another way of acting [that is] more advantageous to men, and at the same time equally worthy of his attributes.[32]

Evidently, Malebranche was able to please neither the Jesuits, at one extreme, nor the Jansenists, at the other: for the Jesuits, Malebranche's God saves too few men, while for the Jansenists, he saves too many – and would apparently save all, if his generality and simplicity did not forbid it. (As Ginette Dreyfus has correctly said in her helpful *La Volonté selon Malebranche*, 'God wills to save all men, but wisdom forbids him to act in such a way that they would actually be saved.'[33] Generality, then, 'saves' God, though it fails to save all men.)

According to Malebranche, the theodicy problems that generality and simplicity of will are meant to solve *must* have a resolution, because the radical imperfection and evil in the universe are all too real, not merely apparent. If they were merely apparent, one could perhaps appeal to the notion of a mysterious *Dieu caché* whose inscrutable ways discover real good in seeming evil. However, this is not Malebranche's view. 'A monster,' he declares, 'is an imperfect work, whatever may have been God's purpose in creating it.'

Some philosophers, perverted by an extravagant metaphysics, come and tell me that God wills evil as positively and directly as the good; that he truly only wills the beauty of the universe...[and]...that the world is a harmony in which monsters are a necessary dissonance; that God wants sinners as well as the just; and that, just as shadows in a painting make its subjects stand out, and give them relief, so too the impious are absolutely necessary in the work of God, to make virtue shine in men of good will.[34]

Those who reason along these lines, in Malebranche's view, are trying to resolve moral dilemmas by appealing to aesthetic similes; but the method will not serve. 'Shadows are necessary in a painting and dissonances in music. Thus it is necessary that women abort and produce an infinity of monsters. What a conclusion!' He ends by insisting, 'I do not agree that there is evil only in appearance.' Hence, *volonté générale* alone, which wills (positively) the good and only *permits* evil as the unavoidable consequence of general and simple laws, is the sole avenue of escape from theodicy problems if one calls evil 'real.' For Malebranche, as for Rousseau in the following century, only *généralité* is positively good and truly justifiable.[35]

Another of the aspects of *volonté générale* that Malebranche's critics found distressing was the possibility that it had been derived or extracted from a Cartesian notion of general laws of uniform motion (in physics) and simply grafted onto the realm of grace.[36] This suspicion was borne out by a careful reading of some passages from *Nature et grâce*. In the *Premier Discours of the Traité*, Malebranche finds a parallel between generaility in nature and in grace, but he *begins* with nature, and finds in grace no more than a kind of analogue to nature. 'Just as one has no right to be annoyed by the fact that rain falls in the sea, where it is useless,' Malebranche argues, so also one has no right 'to complain of the apparent irregularity according to which grace is given to men.' Useless rain and useless grace both derive from 'the regularity with which God acts,' from 'the simplicity of the laws which he follows.' Malebranche reinforces the nature-grace parallel, in which nature seems to be the model for grace, by calling grace a 'heavenly rain which sometimes falls on hardened hearts, as well as on prepared souls.'[37] This horticultural language, of course – which Malebranche himself claimed to have used primarily to persuade Cartesians, not Scholastic theologians[38] – did nothing to dispel the suspicion of traditionalists like Bossuet that Cartesian generality and uniformity might be used in radical ways, to the detriment of traditional teachings about grace based on Scripture and patristic writings. This kind of suspicion – best expressed by Bossuet himself when he says, in a letter dealing with Malebranchism, that he sees 'a great struggle against the Church being prepared in the name of Cartesian philosophy'[39] – was certainly not relieved by Malebranche's insistence that 'what Moses tells us in *Genesis* is so obscure' that the beginning of the world can be explained *à la Descartes* better than any other way.[40] 'Obscurity' is no more welcome than 'anthropology' or 'as if.'

The fear of orthodox Christian moralists that Malebranche had permitted a Cartesian physics to invade and infect the sphere of metaphysics, including ethics, was not wholly groundless. In the *Recherche de la vérité*, Malebranche 'Cartesianizes' everything, not least human volition and action:

> Just as the author of nature is the universal cause of all the movements which are in matter, it is also him who is the general cause [*cause générale*] of all the natural inclinations which are in minds. And just as all movements proceed in a straight line [*en ligne droite*], if there are no foreign and particular causes which determine them, and which change them into curved lines through their opposing forces; so too the inclinations which we receive from God are right [*droites*], and

they could not have any other end than the possession of the
good and of truth if there were not any foreign cause, which
determined the impression of nature towards bad ends.[41]

Like Kant a century later, here Malebranche is playing with the
different senses of 'droit' (meaning both 'straight' and 'right') and of
'curved' (which can mean 'crooked' in a moral sense).[42]   (This same
kind of playing can be found in Rousseau's most famous single
assertion about general will: 'La volonté générale est toujours droite,
mais le jugement qui la guide n'est pas toujours éclairé.'[43]) However,
the key point in connection with Malebranche is that the language of
Cartesian physics has been imposed on morality and psychology;
however briefly, Malebranche resembles Hobbes in accounting for
everything in terms of general *motion*.[44]   Moreover that *généralité*, in
Malebranche, always has supreme weight: if the God of Pascal and
Arnauld permanently abandons a primitive *volonté générale* to save
'all' in favor of a very particular pity for the elect, Malebranche's God
moves as quickly as possible away from an embarrassingly
particularistic Creation and toward generality and simplicity of willing.

IV

Some of the contemporary opponents of Malebranche –
particularly the orthodox Cartesian Pierre Régis – thought that the
notion of a just and justifiable divine *volonté générale* was 'political' in
a wholly bad sense, that Malebranche had confused divine governance
with ordinary human governance and hence had politicized theology.
'I shall not say,' Régis observes, 'that God acts by *volontés générales*,
or by *volontés particulières*, because these two kinds of will cannot be
suitable to a perfect being.'   If God acted only through *volontés
générales*, this would mean 'that he willed things only in a general
way, without descending to anything particular, as a king governs a
kingdom through general laws, not having the power to guide each
subject.'   A mere king falls back on general laws and *volontés
générales*...because these *volontés* suppose an impotence in God
which I cannot attribute to him.'   Since the notion that God operates
through *volontés particulières* is no better, in Régis's view ('it would
follow that the nature of God would be composed of as many different
wills as there are particular things which God wills, which is repugnant
to his simplicity'), it must be the case that 'God acts by a simple,
eternal and immutable will which embraces indivisibly and in a single
act everything that is and will be.'[45]

Malebranche, as it happens, had an answer to this kind of charge. In the seventh of his *Méditations chrétiennes et métaphysiques* (1683), he warns that when one says that God 'permits certain natural disorders, such as the generation of monsters, the violent death of a good man, or something similar,' one must not imagine that there is an autonomous 'nature' to which God has given some of his power and that acts independently of God, 'in the same way that a prince lets ministers act, and permits disorders which he cannot stop.' God *could* stop all 'disorders' (though a prince cannot) by acting through a multiplicity of *volontés particulières*, which would remedy all particular evils. Acting in this fashion, however, would derogate from the simplicity of his ways; God, Malebranche argues, 'does good because he wants his work to be perfect,' and he *permits* (rather than *does*) evil not because he 'positively and directly' wills it but because 'he wants his manner of acting to be simple, regular, uniform and constant, because he wants his conduct to be worthy of him and to wear visibly the character of his attributes.'[46] Thus, for Malebranche, to act by *volontés générales* and general laws does not manifest a quasi-human impotence at all: God can will anything, but acting through *volontés particulières* would not be worthy of him. What he can do is simply a question of power; what he actually wills is a question of wisdom and justice.

If there were critics of Malebranche who claimed that he had illegitimately thought of God as a mere earthly king, there were others who thought that political analogies were, in themselves, perfectly acceptable, and that Malebranche had simply pitched upon false ones. In his *Réflexions sur le système de la nature et de la grâce* (1685), Antoine Arnauld argues that 'there is no contradiction whatever [in the fact] that God wills by a *volonté absolue et particulière* the contrary of what he wills *en générale* by an antecedent will, just as a good king wills by an antecedent will that all his subjects live contentedly, though by a consequent will he executes those who disturb public tranquility by murders and violence.'[47] In Arnauld's view, Malebranche's theory of general justice suffers from the defect of virtually equating *volonté générale*, general law, wisdom, justice, and 'the simplest means'; these terms, according to Arnauld, are not equivalent, and what 'wisdom' requires (e.g., the remedying of particular evils) may not be attainable by 'the simplest means' – either for God or for a human ruler.[48]

For Arnauld, Malebranche's fatal confusion is the conflation of general will and general law; in fact, the operation of a general law may contain a divine *volonté particulière*. In 'proving' this, Arnauld has recourse to Scripture, which Malebranche had minimized. 'If one considers a particular effect,' Arnauld begins in the *Réflexions philosophiques et théologiques*, 'and if one finds nothing but conformity to general laws of nature, one has reason to say, with respect to this effect, that God has acted according to general laws.' However, since this particular effect has many 'remote causes,' one would have to be assured that there has never been a particular divine intervention in this causal sequence before one could say absolutely that any particular effect was '*only* a consequence of the general laws of nature.' One would have, in short, to be omniscient. Now, who, Arnauld asks triumphantly, can 'assure us of this, without a prodigious temerity, and without ruining the faith we have in Providence?'[49]

Arnauld's criticisms finally brought Malebranche to argue only that God 'ordinarily' acts by *volontés générales* and 'not often' by *volontés particulières*.[50] This grudging admission opened the door, however narrowly, to Fénelon's point that 'not often' is an indeterminate notion, that the frequency of *volontés particulières* must be relative to what 'wisdom' requires.[51] And this may be why Malebranche uses the notion of *volonté générale* somewhat sparingly in his later works.[52]

V

In his last work, the *Réflexions sur la prémotion physique*, published in the year of his death (1715), Malebranche found an opportunity to show that his notions of *volonté générale* and general law have a general moral significance that can be used in refuting theories of justice that rely primarily on sovereign power, such as Hobbes's. The *Réflexions* were a commentary on Laurent Boursier's quasi-Jansenist *De l'action de Dieu sur les créatures* (1713) – a large section of which attempted to refute Malebranche's theory of the divine *modus operandi*. In *De l'action de Dieu* Boursier treats God as a 'sovereign' whose will is unrestricted by any necessity to act only through general laws ('God has willed [the world] thus, because he willed it')[53] and argues that Malebranche's notion of divine wisdom renders God 'impotent.'[54] 'The sovereign who governs', Boursier claims, whether God or a prince, 'causes inferiors to act as he wills.' He does this through 'command': 'He interposes his power in order to determine them.' And 'inferiors,' for their part, act only 'because they are excited and determined by the prince...they act in consequence of his determination.'[55]

Since God is a powerful sovereign who has willed the world to be what it is simply 'because he has willed it,' one cannot say that he prefers a Malebranchian generality of 'the simplest means,' or, indeed, that he prefers anything at all; the 'greatness and majesty of the Supreme Being' must make us realize that 'everything that he can will with respect to what is outside himself' is 'equal' to him. Malebranche, Boursier complains, does not see that God can equally will whatever is in his power: 'What an idea of God! He wishes, and he does not

62

accomplish; he does not like monsters, but he makes them; he does not attain the perfection which he desires in his works: he cannot fashion a work without defects...his wisdom limits his power. A strange idea of God! An impotent being, an unskilled workman, a wisdom based on constraint, a sovereign who does not do what he wills, an unhappy God.[56]

In his response to Boursier's theory of sovereignty based on will, command, and power, Malebranche actually abandons the terms *volonté générale* and *volonté particulière* (conceivably because of the constant criticisms of Régis, Arnauld et al.), but he does not abandon the concepts for which the terms stood; thus, *volonté générale* and general law become 'eternal law,' while *volonté particulière becomes volonté absolue et bizarre* (which is more striking still). 'My present design,' Malebranche says, 'is to prove that God is essentially wise, just and good...that his *volontés* are not at all purely arbitrary –that is to say that they are not wise and just simply because he is all-powerful...but because they are regulated by the eternal law...a law which can consist only in the necessary immutable relations which are among the attributes and perfections which God encloses in his essence.' The ideas that we have of wisdom, justice, and goodness 'are quite different from those that we have of omnipotence.' To say that the *volontés* of God are 'purely arbitrary,' that 'no reason can be given for his *volontés*, except his *volontés* themselves,' and that everything that he wills and does is just, wise, and good because he is omnipotent and has a 'sovereign domain' over his creatures – is 'to leave the objections of libertines in all their force.'[57]

The notion that God wills in virtue of eternal law, not simply through the bare possession of sovereign domain, leads Malebranche to a criticism of Hobbes (and Locke) that is an interesting expansion of his notion of *volonté générale*. 'If,' Malebranche says, 'God were only omnipotent, and if he were like princes who glory more in their power than in their nature,' then 'his sovereign domain, or his independence, would give him a right to everything, or he would not act as [an] all-powerful [being].' If this were true of God, then 'Hobbes, Locke and several others would have discovered the true foundations of morality: authority and power giving, without reason, the right to do whatever one wills, when one has nothing to fear.' This legal-positivist view of either human or divine justice Malebranche characterizes as 'mad', and those who attribute this mode of operation to God 'apparently prefer force, the law of brutes (that which has granted to the lion an empire over the animals), to reason.'[58]

However unfair this may be to Hobbes, and still more to Locke – though at least Hobbes does actually say, in chapter 31 of *Leviathan*, that 'irresistible power' carries with it a right to 'dominion[59] – Malebranche's last work shows that he thought that rule through *volontés* that are *particulières* or *absolues* or (even) *bizarres* was wrong in either human or divine governance, and that rule through eternal laws that are of general validity is right. Of course, Malebranche was not alone in this; since Descartes' time a controversy has raged over the question of whether there *are* any eternal laws that God 'finds' in his understanding and 'follows' in his volitions[60] Leibniz (following Plato's *Euthyphro*)[61] put forward a theory of general, non-arbitrary divine justice in his *Théodicée* (1710) that was very close to Malebranche's and criticized Hobbes along (roughly) Malebranchian lines in his *Opinion on the Principles of Pufendorf*.[62] Thus, arguments against Hobbism based on the notion that there are eternal laws of justice which keep divine will from being 'willful' were certainly not scarce at the turn of the eighteenth century; and Malebranche was in perfect accord with Leibniz in disputing Hobbes (and Descartes) on this point.

In connection with his doctrine that God never operates through a *volonté* that is *absolue* or *bizarre*, but only through love of the eternal law, which is 'co-eternal' with him, Malebranche designs one of the strikingly imaginative stage settings that even Voltaire found impressive:

> If God were only all-powerful, or if he gloried only in his omnipotence, without the slightest regard for his other attributes – in a word, without consulting his consubstantial law, his lovable and inviolable law – how strange his plans would be! How could we be certain that, through his omnipotence, he would not, on the first day, place all of the demons in heaven, and all the saints in hell, and a moment after annihilate all that he had done! Cannot God, qua omnipotent, create each day a million planets, make new worlds, each more perfect than the last, and reduce them each year to a grain of sand?[63]

Fortunately, according to Malebranche, though God is in fact all-powerful and 'does whatever he wills to do,' nonetheless he does not will to do anything except 'according to the immutable order of justice.' This is why Malebranche insists, in four or five separate passages of the *Réflexions sur la prémotion physique*, that St. Paul always said 'O altitudo divitiarum Sapientiae et Scientiae Dei' and never 'O altitudo voluntatis Dei.' Will can be willful, if its only attribute is power, and that attribute is the one that Boursier (and Hobbes) wrongly endow with excessive weight.[64]

Despite some disagreements with Malebranche, Leibniz could send a copy of the *Théodicée* to the Oratorian in the confident belief that most of it would prove congenial, and Malebranche's acknowledgement of Leibniz's present ('you prove quite well...that God...must choose the best') showed Leibniz to be right[65] A shared Augustinian Platonism and love of eternal mathematical order formed the *rapport* between Malebranche and Leibniz; and, if Malebranche was a more nearly orthodox Cartesian than his Hannoverian correspondent, even the Oratorian shared Leibniz's distaste for the Cartesian notion that God wills to create mathematical, logical, and moral truth *ex nihilo*.[66]

VI

What is the relation between the 'general will' of God and the 'occasionalism' for which Malebranche is celebrated? That there must be some such *rapport* is evident in *Nature et grâce* itself; Malebranche opens the *Second Discours* by observing that, 'since God alone acts immediately and by himself in minds, and produces in them all the different modifications of which they are capable, it is only he who diffuses light in us, and inspires in us certain feelings which determine our different volitions.' Adding that God alone is the 'true cause,' Malebranche concludes that 'since the general cause [God] acts by laws or by *volontés générales*, and since his action is lawful, constant and uniform, it is absolutely necessary that there be some occasional cause which determines the efficacy of these laws, and which serves to establish them.'[67] If occasional or second causes – for example, human beings – did not act *particularly*, then there would be no relation between general laws and particular actions. Indeed, in one of his defenses of *Nature et grâce*, Malebranche even insists that God cannot act by the simplest means or by general laws until there are occasional causes that determine the efficacy of divine *volontés générales*.[68] Obviously, these causes must be established by creative divine *volontés particulières*; but, since such willings are 'base' and 'servile', God abandons them as soon as generality and simplicity become available.[69]

What, then, is the role of occasionalism in relation to general will? Originally – that is, in orthodox Cartesianism – occasionalism was only a theory of perception and of will: if the essence of body is extension and the essence of mind is thought, then mind and body cannot 'modify' each other, since thought is not a modification of extension and extension is not a modification of thought.[70] Given a strict mind-body dualism, the obvious question is, How can minds 'perceive,' if perception is viewed as a physical modification of the eye or the ear, as motion 'in' a sense organ (as in Hobbes's bawdy insistence that 'there is no conception in a man's mind, which hath not...been begotten upon the organs of sense')[71] and how can minds 'move bodies – through 'volition' – if thought cannot modify extended substances? The obvious answer for an occasionalist must be that so-called 'perception' is not *really* a modification of mind by sense matter, and that volition is not *really* efficacious; instead, God presents to the mind the *idea* of the thing 'seen' on the *occasion* of its being 'seen', just as he moves bodies (for us, as it were) on the occasion of our 'willing.' This occasionalism does not, of course, require a constantly intervening *Deus ex machina* who scurries about the universe giving efficacy to occasional causes. Indeed, Malebranche's theory of *general* law means that God has established a permanent, general relation between mind and body, so that these naturally unrelated substances operate in constant conjunction. Thus, for Malebranche, whenever one wills to move his arm, it moves – thanks to a constant, general (though non-natural) conjunction between mind and body, which God has established by a general will. 'It is only God,' he insists in the *Conversations chrétiennes*, 'who can act in the [human] soul...through his general will which makes the natural order.[72]

It was not simply in order to be a Cartesian that Malebranche was an occasionalist; indeed, his motivation was as much theological as philosophical. Malebranche's view was that the attribution of independent causal efficacy to non-divine being is *impious*; to make that clear, he employed the political idea of 'sovereignty.' 'The idea of a sovereign power is the idea of a sovereign divinity,' Malebranche urges in *De la recherche de la vérité*, 'and the idea of a subordinate divine in all the bodies that surround us, when one admits...real beings capable of producing certain effects by the [causal] force of their nature; and one thus enters insensibly into the sentiment of the pagans.' It is true, he adds, that 'faith corrects us' by reminding us of the Pauline notion that *in God* we 'move' and 'have our being'; nonetheless, if one reads too much Aristotle, 'the mind is pagan' even if 'the heart is Christian.' This is why one must prefer St. Augustine, 'this great saint [who] recognized that the body cannot act upon the soul, and that nothing can be above the soul, except God.[73] It is no wonder that Malebranche read Descartes as an Augustinian, and the Aristotle-loving Scholastics as thinly veiled pagans.

One of the best brief and nontechnical accounts of occasionalism is offered by Malebranche in the *Traité de morale*:

> The [human] mind can be immediately related to God alone...for mind cannot be related to body, except by being united to God himself. It is certain for a thousand reasons that when I suffer, for example, the pain of being pricked, it is God who acts in me, in consequence nonetheless of laws of the union of soul and body...But the body itself cannot be united to the mind, nor the mind to the body. They have no relation between them, nor any creature [a relation] to any other: I mean a relation of [true] causality...It is God who does everything. His will is the link of all unions.[74]

All of this, of course, is merely an elaboration of Malebranche's first statement of occasionalist doctrine in book 6 of *Recherche de la vérité*:

> There is only one true God, and one cause who is truly a cause: and one must not imagine that what precedes an effect is the true cause of it. God cannot communicate his power to creatures, if we follow the light of reason: there cannot be [many] true causes, there cannot be gods. But even if he could do this, we cannot conceive that he would will it. Bodies, minds, pure intelligences – none of these can do anything. It is he who has made minds that enlightens and moves them...It is, finally, the author of our being who executes our wills.[75]

Like the Cartesians, Malebranche begins by viewing occasionalism as a theory of perception and of volition. In the end, however, occasionalism serves a huge range of functions, some of them non-Cartesian. As a theory of knowledge and perception, Malebranchian occasionalism leads to the famous idea that 'we see all things in God';[76] as a theory of volition, it holds that God 'moves our arm' ('it seems to me quite certain that the will of minds is not capable of moving the smallest body that there is in the world');[77] as part of the theory of grace, it maintains that the 'human soul' of Jesus Christ is the occasional cause of the distribution of grace to particular persons.[78] (It is this last element that is non-Cartesian, or at least extra-Cartesian, since Descartes was politic enough to say next to nothing about grace.)[79]

One can begin, as does Malebranche himself, with knowledge and perception. The most important passage in which he treats the moral significance of the notion that 'we see all things in God' is a remarkable commentary on St. Augustine in yet another of his defenses of *Nature et grâce* against Antoine Arnauld – this time, the *Trois Lettres* of 1685. Malebranche begins by allowing that St. Augustine himself did not claim to find *all* things in God: 'I realized,' he grants, 'that this Father spoke only of truths and of eternal laws, of the objects of the sciences, such as arithmetic, geometry, morality; and that he did not urge that one saw in God things which are corruptible and subject to change, as are all the things that surround us.' Malebranche himself does not claim that one sees corruptible and changing things in God; 'to speak exactly, one sees in God only the essences' of things, and those essence or *ideas* of things alone are 'immutable, necessary and eternal.' One sees in God only 'that which represents these things to the mind,...that which renders them intelligible.'[80] As Malebranche put the matter in his correspondence of 1714 with Dortous de Mairan, 'I see immediately [in God] only the idea, and not the *ideatum*, and I am persuaded that the idea has been for an eternity, without [any] *ideatum*.'[81] Corruptible things are problematical because they change, though their essence does not, but incorruptible, unchanging things one sees *simply* in God. 'One can see only in an immutable nature, and in eternal wisdom, all the truths which, by their nature, are immutable and eternal.' It would not be difficult to prove, as St. Augustine did, that 'there would no longer be any certain science, any demonstrated truths, any assured difference between the just and the unjust – in a word, truths and laws which are necessary and common to all minds – if that which all intelligences contemplate were not...by its nature absolutely immutable, eternal and necessary.'[82] All of this, of course, simply reinforces the view that God and men 'see' the same speculative and practical truths.

Malebranche maintained this view of the moral importance of a 'vision' in which nothing is seen, which is not a modification of mind by body, to the end of his philosophical career. In the fragmentary remains of a letter of 1713 to Fénelon, he argues that 'if the mind forms its ideas by a vital act,' and if 'our ideas as distinguished from our perceptions are only chimeras,' then Pyrrhonism will be established. If *all* ideas are simply mind modified by matter, then 'Hobbes and Locke, authors greatly esteemed by many men, will be right.[83] And if they *are* right, 'there will be no more true, nor false, immutably such; neither just, nor unjust, neither science nor morality.' If empirical notions of perception and knowledge carry the day, 'St. Augustine will pass for a fanatical Platonist' who has taught his 'subtle atheism' to Malebranche himself. In Malebranche's view, Hobbes and Locke simply extend the theory of Aristotle (and of his 'impious commentator' Averroës) that 'seeing objects is accomplished by means of impressed species...by the power of an active intellect which presents [ideas] to a passive intellect.' But this, Malebranche insists, is a 'fiction of men who wanted to discuss what they did not understand.[84]

Locke, for his part, thought Malebranche's 'vision in God' just as impious as Malebranche thought Locke's 'sense perception.' In his 'Examination of Père Malebranche's Opinion of Seeing All Things in God' Locke argues, 'God has given me an understanding of my own; and I should think it presumptuous in me to suppose I apprehended anything by God's understanding, saw with his eyes, or shared of his knowledge.' He goes on to ask (and this bears directly on Malebranche's notion that we see moral *rapports de perfection* in God), 'In which of the perfections of God does a man see the essence of a horse or an ass, of a serpent or a dove, of hemlock or parsley?' Locke confesses that he himself cannot see the essence of any of these things 'in any of the perfections of God.' It is perfectly true, he goes on, that 'the perfections that are in God are necessary and unchangeable.' However, it is not true that 'the ideas that are...in the understanding of God...can be seen by us'; it is still less true that 'the perfections that are in God represent to us the essences of things that are out of God.[85]   Here Locke strikes on a real difficulty in Malebranchism – namely, that Malebranche calls a 'perfection' in God what he ought to have called a mere *idea* in God (since it is hard to see how a perfection can 'represent' an imperfect thing, though an *idea* of an imperfect thing remains quite conceivable).

In another criticism of Malebranche, Locke adds that the Malebranchian notion that God cannot communicate to creatures the powers of real perception and real volition sets 'very narrow bounds to the power of God, and, by pretending to extend it, takes it away.' He concludes his assault on occasionalism with a moral objection:

> The creatures cannot produce any idea, any thought in man. How then comes he to perceive or think? God upon the occasion of some motion in the optic nerve, exhibits the colour of a marygold or a rose to his mind. How came that motion in his optic nerve? On occasion of the motion of some particles of light striking on the retina, God producing it, and so on. And so whatever a man thinks, God produces the thought: let it be infidelity, murmuring or blasphemy.[86]

For Locke, then, *tout en Dieu* is a moral enormity; for Malebranche it is a moral necessity.

VII

Just as, for Malebranche, there is no 'empirical' perception in the Hobbesian or Lockean sense, so too there is little notion of human will – 'little' rather than 'no' because of an obvious problem: if men are merely the occasional causes of their own actions, in what sense are they free agents who are accountable for good action, for choosing order or *le bien général* in preference to *amour-propre* and *les biens particulièrs*?[87] As Malebranche himself says in *Recherche de la vérité*, 'without liberty there are neither good nor bad actions.'[88] (To be sure, this is not quite the problem for Malebranche that it would be for a moralist like Kant, who holds that a good will is the only *unqualifiedly* good thing on earth.)[89] Still, according to Malebranche, men are free and hence possibly responsible in the sense that they must 'consent' to a 'motive'; God inclines men through Augustinian-Pascalian *délectation* toward *le bien* or order *en général*, and one must feel this delight before consent is possible.[90] (or, as Malebranche put it in an untranslatable passage, 'il faut sentir...avant que de consentir.')[91] Nevertheless, one can suspend one's consent, can be motivated by a *délectation* without being irresistibly or 'invincibly' determined by it.

Hence, Malebranche's most adequate definition of will, at least in his later work, is 'consenting to a motive.'[92] The essence of liberty, he argues in *Réflexions sur la prémotion physique* 'consists in a true power...which the soul has, to suspend or to give its consent to motives, which naturally follow interesting perceptions.'[93] In suspending one's consent to an interesting or even delectable motive, however, one does not actually *cause* anything to happen – as Malebranche is careful to make clear in the first 'Eclaircissement' of the *Recherche de la vérité*. If we allow a *délectation* that is *déreglé* (such as 'concupiscence') to overwhelm us, and if we fail to suspend our consent to this motive in favor of order or *rapports de perfection*, what do we actually do?

> Nothing. We love a false good, which God does not make us love by an invincible impression. We cease to look for the true good...The only thing we do is stop ourselves, put ourselves at rest. It is through an act, no doubt, but through an immanent act which produces nothing physical in our substance...that is, in a word, through an act which does nothing and which makes the general cause [God] do nothing...for the repose of the soul, like that of the body, has no force or physical efficacy.[94]

This somewhat peculiar doctrine, in which human willing is 'an act, no doubt,' but one that 'produces nothing physical,' is necessitated by Malebranche's view that God alone is a *true* cause, but that, at the same time, men must in *some* way be accountable for their volitions.[95] In his last work, the *Réflexions sur la prémotion physique*, Malebranche tries especially hard to make this doctrine plausible by drawing a fine distinction between two different powers or activities in the human soul. He begins by asserting that 'the *willing* power of the soul, so to speak, its desire to be happy, its movement toward the good in general' is the first power or activity; but it is a power that is 'certainly the effect of the Creator's will.' This power, then, is 'only the action of God' *in* the soul; it is therefore 'like that of created bodies in motion...whose moving force...depends on the action of God.' It is a power *in* us, indeed, but it is not 'ours'; it is, to recall a favorite Malebranchism, *en nous sans nous*.[96]

For Malebranche, it is the second power of the soul that is more interesting with regard to human moral responsibility, because it is really ours: 'The second power or activity of the soul...which constitutes the essence of liberty...consists in a true power, not to produce in itself, through its own efficacity, any new modifications; but it consists in a true power which the soul has, to suspend or give its consent to motives, which naturally follow interesting perceptions.'[97] Will, then, understood as 'consent to a motive', consists in passively permitting that motive to operate.

Even if one can perhaps characterize this passive consent as involving 'rien de physic,' can one say the same of suspending a motive (such as concupiscence) while one searches for order and *rapports de perfection*? Do 'suspending' and 'searching' involve *rien de physic*? Malebranche seems to be caught between God as the only true cause and the wish to avoid a 'Spinozistic' determinism in which men are unfree 'modes' of the divine substance, and will is therefore an illusion; hence his account of will as both passive and active (or perhaps suspended on a line between the passive and the active). Malebranche thought that he was avoiding one of the chief errors of Jansenism – namely, viewing the *délectation* of 'efficacious' grace as irresistible. An irresistible motive, which one cannot suspend or resist without contradiction, truly destroys the possibility of freely loving order and *le bien général* and of meritoriously abandoning *les biens particuliers*, such as the pleasures of the body, which has no natural *rapport* with the mind.[98]

Locke thought Malebranche's attenuated notion of 'will' even more impious, if possible, than the notion of 'vision in God': 'A man cannot move his arm or his tongue; he has no power; only upon occasion, the man willing it, God moves it...This is the hypothesis that clears doubts, and brings us at last to the religion of Hobbes and Spinoza, by resolving all, even the thoughts and will of men, into an irresistible fatal necessity.'[99] It is ironic, of course, that in the second edition (1694) of his *Essay Concerning Human Understanding* Locke himself defines human liberty as the capacity to 'suspend' any 'particular' desire while one searches for happiness 'in general,' for the true good.[100] Here there is a strong Locke-Malebranche 'relation' – strong enough to make one wonder whether, despite Locke's general hostility to Malebranchism, that doctrine did not (particularly) affect the Lockean notions of liberty and will. This *rapport* is at its clearest in the account of the alterations to the 1694 edition of the *Essay* that Locke provided in a letter to his friend Molyneux, the Dublin *savant*, in August 1693: 'All that we desire is only to be happy. But though this general desire of happiness operates constantly and invariably in us, yet the satisfaction of any particular desire can be suspended from determining the will to any subservient action, till we have maturely examined whether the particular apparent good we then desire make a part of our real happiness.'[101]

Like Malebranche, Locke speaks of a 'general' desire for happiness; this general desire operates 'constantly and invariably' (like all Malebranchian general laws). Moreover, all 'particular' goods may be merely 'apparent' and not part of 'real' or 'general' happiness. In book 2 chapter 28 of the *Essay*, entitled 'Of Other Relations,' Locke argues that 'there is another kind of relation, which is the conformity or disagreement men's voluntary actions have to a rule to which they are referred...which, I think, may be called *moral relation*'; he goes on to call three 'sorts' of moral relation *laws* (divine, civil and 'of reputation').[102]   Despite a seemingly strong relation between the two thinkers, however, Locke's final view may well be that Malebranche has no grounds for insisting on the real   existence of human 'will' and hence is not entitled to speak of 'suspension' – even as an 'immanent' act which 'does nothing', produces *rien de physic*.

VIII

What finally matters, for Malebranche, is that there be *will* – divine and human – but that it not be willful; like Leibniz in the *Discourse on Metaphysics*, Malebranche wants to say that *stat pro ratione voluntas* is 'properly the motto of a tyrant.'[104]   This non-willful voluntarism is at its clearest in Malebranche's very last work, the *Prémotion physique*, in which 'moral relations are not simple *truths*, but...also have the force of *laws*; for one must esteem all things in proportion as they are estimable and lovable; in proportion as they participate in the divine perfections. And since the nature of God is immutable and necessary, and since God can neither see nor will that two times two be equal to five, how can it fail to be perceived that God can neither see nor will that the idea of man which he has participate less in his perfections than that of the beast? that, as a consequence, he can neither see nor will that it be just to prefer, or rather will to prefer, one's horse to one's coachman, simply because one can or wants to? Power or will adds nothing to the eternal law, to the relations of perfection which subsist between the eternal and immutable ideas.'[105]

At the end of his life, Malebranche's Augustine-conveyed Platonism is almost as pure as Leibniz'; both have taken the *Euthyphro* to heart. For Malebranche, in the end, will is necessary, but not sufficient: *volonté* is naturally *générale* in God, and that generality remains an object of human striving.

N.B.: This essay is adapted, with permission, from the author's *The General Will Before Rousseau*, Princeton University Press, 1986 (2nd ed. 1988).

Notes

1.   Malebranche, *Traité de la nature et de la grâce*, ed. G. Dreyfus, in *Oeuvres complètes* (Paris: Vrin, 1958), 'Premier Discours.'

2.   Ibid., 'Troisième Discours'.

3. Malebranche, *Recherche de la vérité*, in OCM III, pp. 506, 508. On the question of how far Malebranche is an orthodox Cartesian, see Ferdinand Alquié, *Le Cartésianisme de Malebranche* (Paris: Vrin, 1974), pp. 243ff.

4. Cited in Emile Bréhier, 'Les Lectures malebranchistes de J. J. Rousseau,' *Revue internatonale de philosophie* 1 (1938-1939), pp. 113-114.

5. Malebranche, *Nature et grâce*, in OCM V, p. 47: God is obliged 'to act always in a way worthy of him, in simple, general, constant and uniform ways.'

6. Ibid., pp. 147, 148.

7. Ibid., p. 63.

8. Ibid., p. 166.

9. Malebranche, *Nature et grâce*, in OCM V, p. 32.

10. Ibid., pp. 63-64, 166 (*inter alia*).

11. Ibid., pp. 50-51.

12. Ibid., p. 47.

13. Leibniz, *Theodicy*, p. 62. For a fuller treatment of Leibniz's notion of divine justice, see the author's 'An Unpublished MS of Leibniz on the Allegiance Due to Sovereign Powers', in *Journal of the History of Philosophy 11* (July 1973), pp. 324ff.

14. Malebranche, *Nature et grâce*, in OCM V, p. 46.

15. Ibid., p. 63.

16. Malebranche, *Traité de morale*, ed. M. Adam, in OCM XI, pp. 31-33.

17. Malebranche, *Réponse au livre de Mr. Arnau[l]d, Des vrayes et des fausses idées*, in OCM VI-VII, p. 43.

18. Malebranche, *Nature et grâce*, in OCM V, pp. 61-62.

19. If one examines the 1684 edition of *Nature et grâce* (Rotterdam: Chez Reinier Leers, 1684), one finds that all the additions to the 1680 text are set in italic type.

20. Pascal, *Écrits sur la grâce*, in *Oeuvres de Blaise Pascal*, ed. L. Brunschvicg (Paris: Hachette, 1914), vol. 11, pp. 135-140.

21. St. Augustine, trans. Arnauld (Paris: 1644), *Correction et grâce*, p. 7.

22. Malebranche, *Nature et grâce*, in OCM V, pp. 67-68.

23. Pierre Jurieu, *L'Esprit de M. Arnau[l]d* (Deventer: Jean Colombius, 1684), pp. 80ff., esp. p. 80: 'Je ne scay le P. Malebranche a eu un ami assez fidele, pour lui apprendre qu'il n'y a jamais eu de Livre plus généralement désapprouvé que [*Nature et grâce*].'

24. Malebranche, *Nature et grâce*, in OCM V, p. 204.

25. Ibid., p. 180.

26. Malebranche, *Réponse à une dissertation de M. Arnauld contre un eclaircissement de la nature et de la grâce*, in OCM VI-VII, pp. 591-592.

27. Malebranche, *Nature et grâce*, in OCM V, pp. 47-48.

28. Cited in Ginette Dreyfus, *La Volonté selon Malebranche* (Paris: Vrin, 1958), p. 114.

29. Malebranche, *Réponse au livre I des réflexions philosophiques*, in OCM VIII-IX, p. 721. Cf. p. 722: 'S'il [Dieu] avoit une volonté absolue de sauver tous les hommes, sans avoir egard à la simplicité des moyens, il est certain qu'il les sauveroit tous.'

30. Malebranche, *Réflexions sur la prémotion physique*, in OCM XVI, p. 118.

31. Leibniz, letter to Malebranche (December 1711), cited in Malebranche, OCM XIX, p. 815.

32. Rodolphe Du Tertre, *Réfutation d'un nouveau système de métaphysique proposé par le Père Malebranche* (Paris: Chez Raymond Mazières, 1715), pp. 275-277. (The only available copy of Du Tertre's work is in the Bibliothèque Nationale, Paris – through whose courtesy the author was able to examine the *Réfutation* in November 1982.) Du Tertre has been an ardent Malebranchian, but was ordered by his Jesuit superiors to relinquish his views; unlike his fellow Jesuit and one-time friend Y. M. André, he followed orders.

33. Dreyfus, *Volonté selon Malebranche*, p. 114.

34. Cited in André Robinet, *Système et existence dans l'oeuvre de Malebranche* (Paris: Vrin, 1965), pp. 104-105.

35. See particularly Alberto Postigliola, 'De Malebranche à Rousseau: Les Apories de la volonté générale et la revanche du 'raisonneur violent', in *Annales de la Société Jean-Jacques Rousseau* (Geneva: Chez A. Jullien, 1980), vol. 39, pp. 134ff.

36. This was the fear of both Arnauld and Bossuet; see note 114.

37. Malebranche, *Nature et grâce*, in OCM V, p. 50.

38. Ibid., p. 7.

39. Bossuet, letter to Marquis d'Allemans (May 1687), in Malebranche, OCM XVIII, p. 445.

40. Malebranche, *Réponse au livre I*, p. 780.

41. Malebranche, *Recherche de la vérité*, p. 45.

42. Immanuel Kant, 'Einleitung in der Rechtslehre,' sec. *E, Die Metaphysik der Sitten*, in *Immanuel Kants Werke*, ed. Ernest Cassirer (Berlin: Bruno Cassirer Verlag, 1922), vol. 7, p. 34.

43. Rousseau, *Du contrat social*, p. 50.

44. See Elisabeth Labrousse, *Pierre Bayle*, vol. 2, pp. 592ff.

45. Pierre-Sylvain Régis, *Cours entier de philosophie ou système général selon les principes de M. Descartes* (Amsterdam: Huguetan, 1691), vol. 1, pp. 92, 93. For a commentary on Régis's thought, see Genevieve Lewis, *Le Problème de l'inconscient et le cartésianisme* (Paris: Presses Universitaires de France, 1950).

46. Malebranche, *Méditations chrétiennes*, pp. 76, 77.

47. Arnauld, *Réflexions philosophiques et théologiques*, in *Oeuvres*, vol. 39, p. 198. For a fine account of Arnauld's criticisms of Malebranche, see Ginette Dreyfus's Introduction to her edition of Malebranche's *Nature et grâce*, pp. 47ff.

48. Arnauld, *Réflexions philosophiques et théologiques*, in *Oeuvres*, pp. 174ff. 'It has never been said that it is not to act by a *volonté particulière*, when one wills each particular effect positively and directly, though in conformity to a general law. Otherwise Jesus Christ, having has a general law which he

always had in view – which was to follow in all things the orders of his father – would have to be said never to have willed, by *volontés particulières*, everything which he did in particular for the redemption of the human race.' One must conclude, therefore, *contra* Malebranche, that 'God acts by *volontés particulières* in consequence of general laws' (p. 175).

49. Ibid., p. 177.

50. Malebranche, *Réponse à une dissertation de M. Arnauld*, pp. 493ff.: 'I believe that God does not often act by *volontés particulières*, and that ordinarily he follows the general laws which he as prescribed for himself.'

51. Fénelon, *Réfutation du système de Père Malebranche*, pp. 258-259: 'But in what consists that which the author [Malebranche] calls 'rarely'? Is there a fatal number of exceptions which God is obliged to use up, beyond which he can will nothing except in accordance with general laws? Would one dare to say this?'

52. Nevertheless, when Malebranche wrote a seventeenth 'Eclaircissement' of *Recherche de la vérité* for the last edition published under his supervision (1712), he still insisted that 'God acts by laws or by *volontés générales.*' For this 'Eclaircissement,' see OCM III, p. 346.

53. Laurent Boursier, *De l'action de Dieu sur les créatures* (Paris: Babuty, 1713), p. 70. (Substantial extracts from Boursier's work are printed as an appendix to Malebranche, OCM XVI, pp. 199ff.)

54. Ibid., p. 76: 'C'est que sa sagesse le rend impuissant.'

55. Ibid., p. 36.

56. Ibid., pp. 47, 79.

57. Malebranche, *Prémotion physique*, pp. 93, 101, 104.

58. Ibid., pp. 93, 98.

59. Hobbes, *Leviathan*, ed. M. Oakeshott (Oxford: Basil Blackwell, 1957), chapter 31, p. 234: 'To those therefore whose power is irresistible, the dominion of all men adhereth naturally by their excellence or power.' As for Locke, Malebranche may be thinking of the passage in *The Reasonableness of Christianity* in which Locke argues that 'those just measures of right and wrong which…[ancient]…philosophy recommended, stood on their true foundations…But where was it that their obligation was thoroughly known and allowed, and they received and acknowledgement of the law-maker, and the great rewards and punishments, for those that would,

or would not obey him' (in *Works of John Locke*, vol. 7, p. 144). Malebranche would not have approved the notion that the 'just measures of right and wrong' derive their whole force from reward, punishment, and obedience.

60.   For a fuller treatment of this point, see Jean-Luc Marion, 'De la création des vérités éternelles au principe de la raison: remarques sur l'anticartésianisme de Spinoza, Malebranche, Leibniz,' in *Dix-septième Siècle*, vol. 37, No. 2, April/June 1985, pp. 143-164; and Geneviève Rodis-Lewis, 'La crèation des vérités éternelles: polémiques sur la création des possibles et sur l'impossible dans l'école cartésienne,' in *Studia Cartesiana* (Amsterdam: Quadratures, 1981), vol. 2, pp. 105-123.

61.   Plato, *Euthyphro* 9E-10E in *Plato: The Collected Dialogues*, ed. E. Hamilton and H. Cairns (New York: Bollingen, 1961), pp. 178-179.

62.   Leibniz, *Principles of Pufendorf*, pp. 64ff: 'Neither the norm of conduct itself, nor the essence of the just, depends on his [God's] free decision, but rather on eternal truths, objects of the divine intellect, which constitute, so to speak, the essence of divinity itself...Justice, indeed, would not be an essential attribute of God, if he himself established justice and law by his free will.' For an appreciation of the limits of Leibniz's Platonism, see the author's 'An Unpublished MS of Leibniz on the Existence of God,' in *Studia Leibnitiana* (Hannover), 1984.

63.   Malebranche, *Prémotion physique*, p. 100.

64.   Ibid., pp. 72, 93, 122, etc.

65.   Cited in Robinet, *Malebranche et Leibniz*, p. 417.

66.   See Alquié, *Cartésianisme de Malebranche*, pp. 226ff.

67.   Malebranche, *Nature et grâce*, in OCM V, pp. 66-67. On Malebranche's occasionalism, see Ginette Dreyfus, *La Volonté selon Malebranche* (Paris: Vrin, 1958), Chapter 6 (Dieu seule cause éfficace), and Robinet, *Système et éxistence*, pp. 27ff. ('passage de la philosophie de l'occasion au système occasionaliste').

68.   Malebranche, *Réponse au livre I des Réflexions philosophiques*, in OCM VIII-IX, p. 780..

69.   Cited in Dreyfus, *Volonté selon Malebranche*, p. 105.

70.   See the excellent notes on Cartesianism by Pierre Costabel that accompany Malebranche, OCM XVII-I, pp. 30-37, 199-236. See also Alquié,

Cartésianisme de Malebranche, pp. 243ff., who shows that Descartes himself cannot be called an orthodox occasionalist. Nonetheless, there are intimations of occasionalism in Descartes' thought; for these see Pierre Clair, 'Louis de La Forge et les origines de l'occasionalisme,' in *Recherches sur le XVIIème siècle* (Paris: CNRS, 1976), vol. 1, pp. 63-72.

71. Thomas Hobbes, *Leviathan*, ed. M. Oakeshott (Oxford: Basil Blackwell, 1957), p. 7. One can wonder how moral 'conceptions' are conceivable at all on this view.

72. Malebranche, *Conversations chrétiennes*, in OCM IV, p. 83.

73. Cited in Alquié, *Malebranche* (Paris: Seghers, 1977), pp. 116, 117.

74. Malebranche, *Traité de morale*, p. 117.

75. Malebranche, *Recherche de la vérité* in OCM II, p. 318.

76. See particularly Gouhier, *Experience religieuse*, pp. 211-243. Gouhier properly lays great weight on the following line from the Dixième Eclaircissement' of the *Recherche*: 'This principle that it is only God who enlightens us, and that he only enlightens us through the manifestation of an immutable and necessary reason or wisdom, seems to me...so absolutely necessary to give to any truth whatsoever a certain and unshakable foundation, that I believe myself indispensably obliged to explain it and to sustain it as far as it is possible for me' (p. 237).

77. Malebranche, *Recherche de la vérité*, in OCM II, pp. 318, 315.

78. Malebranche, *Nature et grâce*, in OCM V, pp. 65-99.

79. See Alquié, *Cartésianisme de Malebranche*, p. 429: 'Le *Traité de la nature et de la grâce* ramène la conduite divine à une action physicienne. Jamais les cartésiens n'avaient osé étendre si loin les principes du mécanisme...[In Malebranche]... l'ordre de la grâce est soumis aux principes de l'occasionalisme et de la simplicité des voies.' As for Descartes himself, he is carefully orthodox (and a little vague) in his letter to Père Mersenne (March 1642): 'Pelagius said that one could do good works and merit eternal life without grace, which was condemned by the Church; as for me, I say that one can know by natural reason that God exists, but I do not therefore say that this natural knowledge merits in itself, and without grace, the supernatural glory that we expect in heaven. For, on the contrary, it is evident that, this glory being supernatural, it requires more than natural powers to merit it' (in Descartes, *Oeuvres et lettres*, ed. André Bridoux [Paris: Pléiade, 1953], p. 1144). By naturalizing the distribution of grace – by making the realm of grace operate through general, simple, uniform,

quasi-physical laws – Malebranche does indeed, as Alquié says, 'extend' the principles of mechanism in a non-Cartesian way.

80. Malebranche, *Trois Lettres touchant la défense de M. Arnauld*, in OCM VI-VII, pp. 199-200. Malebranche says in a footnote that he is relying particularly on Augustine's *De libero arbitrio* and *De trinitate*; Arnauld, by contrast, builds *his* 'Augustinianism' on the late, proto-Jansenist *De correptione et gratia*.

81. In Malebranche, OCM XIX, p. 910.

82. Malebranche, *Trois Lettres*, p. 199.

83. Malebranche, letter to Fénelon, in *Oeuvres complètes*, vol. 19, pp. 842-843. The circumstances surrounding the composition of this letter are given in Yves Marie André, *La Vie du R. P. Malebranche*, pub. Ingold (Geneva: Slatkine, 1970), pp. 355ff.

84. Malebranche, letter to Fénelon, pp. 842-843.

85. Locke, 'An Examination of P. Malebranche's Opinion of Seeing All Things in God,' in *The Works of John Locke* (London: Otridge & Son et al., 1812), vol. 9, pp. 211-255. For a fine commentary on this work, see McCracken, *Malebranche and British Philosophy*, pp. 119ff. See also J. Yolton, *John Locke* (Oxford: Clarendon Press, 1956), p. 98.

86. Locke, 'Remarks upon Some of Mr. Norris's Book, Wherein He Asserts P. Malebranche's Opinion of Our Seeing All Things in God,' in vol. 10, p. 255.

87. See Dreyfus, *Volonté selon Malebranche*, p. 197.

88. Malebranche, *Recherche de la vérité* in OCM III, p. 225: 'If we had no liberty at all, there would be neither future punishments nor recompenses; for without liberty there are neither good nor bad actions: so that religion would be an illusion and a phantom.'

89. Kant, *Fundamental Principles of the Metaphysic of Morals*, trans. T. K. Abbott (Indianapolis: Library of Liberal Arts, 1949), pp. 11-12.

90. Malebranche, *Réflexions sur la prémotion physique*, in *Oeuvres complètes*, vol. 16, pp. 3ff.

91. Ibid., p. 18. Cf. p. 35: 'It is agreed that it is in the feelings and in the movements which God produces in us without us [*en nous sans nous*], that the material of sin consists, and that the formal [cause of sin] consists only

in the consent that one gives: and all this because it does not depend on us to feel, but it does depend on us to consent.'

92. Ibid., p. 50: 'To will is to consent to a motive.'

93. Ibid., p. 47.

94. Malebranche, *Recherche de la vérité*, in OCM III, pp. 24-25.

95. In *Prémotion physique*, p. 45, Malebranche explains the relation between human will and divine general will by urging that 'the immanent acts of the [human] will are inefficacious by themselves…they do not produce the slightest physical change in the soul, and…are only occasional causes, which determine the efficacy…of the *volontés générales* of the all-powerful'.

96. Malebranche, *Prémotion physique*, pp. 46-47. The best commentary on this part of Malebranche's thought is Dreyfus's *Volonté selon Malebranche*, pp. 274-283.

97. Malebranche, *Prémotion physique*, p. 47.

98. Ibid., pp. 8-22.

99. Locke, 'Remarks upon Some of Mr. Norris's Books,' pp. 255-256. For a fuller treatment of Locke's theory of volition, see the author's *Will and Political Legitimacy: A Critical Exposition of Social Contract Theory in Hobbes, Locke, Rousseau, Kant and Hegel* (Cambridge, Mass.: Harvard University Press, 1982), pp. 74-83.

100. Locke, pp. 343ff.

101. In Locke, *Correspondence of John Locke*, ed. E. S. de Beer (Oxford: Clarendon Press, 1979), vol. 4, p. 722.

102. Locke, *Human Understanding*, pp. 471ff.

103. Leibniz, *Discourse on Metaphysics* (1686), Proposition 2.

104. Malebranche, *Réflexions sur la prémotion physique*, in OCM V.

6 Malebranche's Occasionalism and Leibniz's Pre-established Harmony: an 'Easy Crossing' or an Unbridgeable Gap?

STUART BROWN

How far is Leibniz's system of pre-established harmony really different from Malebranche's occasionalism? Philosophers since the late seventeenth century have been puzzled over this question. Even Leibniz, although he declared himself on the subject several times, seems hardly to have offered a consistent answer. He assured Simon Foucher, in 1686, that his system was 'very different'[1] from that of Malebranche. Again, his *New System* implies that he had found occasionalism to be only of negative value[2] in showing what cannot be the case. But, especially in his later writings, he seems to have minimized the differences between himself and Malebranche. For instance, in 1714, he wrote to Nicolas Remond: 'The crossing *["passage "* is the French word] from occasional causes to the pre-established harmony does not seem to be very difficult'.[3] And to Guillaume l'Hôpital he wrote that his new system was 'not so much a reversal as a continuation' (*avancement*) of Malebranche's doctrine[4] His remark in that context that it was to Malebranche that he owed his 'foundations' in this subject could easily be taken to imply that his system of pre-established harmony was no more than a development of or variation on fundamentally Malebranchean themes.

In this paper I shall try to bring out how Leibniz's system did indeed develop from something like occasionalism. I shall argue, however, that Leibniz eventually returned to a basically Scholastic view of natural modalities, one that was radically at variance with an occasionalist view of Nature, as well as his own views in the early to mid 1680s. The story of how Leibniz's philosophy is related to

81

occasionalism is a complex one and has yet to be told in full. Here I can only outline its main features, omitting much of the detail.

Leibniz was still in Paris when the *Recherche de la Vérité* was first published in 1674.[5] From that time on he took a particular interest in Malebranche's writings and the controversies they provoked. He strongly agreed with Malebranche that there are reasons for everything God does, that nothing is due to arbitrary fiat, that there are 'laws of grace' as well as 'laws of nature' and that God's perfections are expressed in His creation.[6] His points of agreement often have a strongly Platonic resonance and it is significant that Leibniz later insisted that his Platonism was 'the part of Father Malebranche's system that I would be happy to see preserved'.[7]

Leibniz's admiration for Malebranche always fell short of discipleship. If he was attracted by many of Malebranche's conclusions he was quick to see when they could not be defended without modification. The *Recherche* began a controversy in which Leibniz's friend, Simon Foucher, played a prominent part, writing a provocative and highly sceptical *Critique*.[8] It is clear from Leibniz's notes on Foucher's defence[9] of his *Critique* that he found the debate a considerable stimulus to his own thought. One remark, indeed, contains the germ of what was to become his own distinctive position. 'Perhaps' (he suggests) 'it is the nature of our soul to be the immediate cause of our perceptions of material things and (perhaps) it is God, the author of all things, who is the cause of the harmony between our thoughts and what is outside us'.[10] Leibniz was to return to this line of thinking. But in 1679 his position seems to have been much closer to that of Malebranche, to whom he wrote: 'I enthusiastically approve of these two propositions that you put forward: namely, that we see all things in God and that bodies do not strictly act on us'.[11] But, as he went on to imply by saying that he had reasons of his own for holding these doctrines, this agreement was not so much a matter of his following Malebranche as of their views converging. Occasionalism of one kind or another was embraced not only by the Cartesians but also by others, like Leibniz, who accepted the mechanical philosophy. Leibniz had for some time been what might be called a semi-occasionalist. He had taken it to be a consequence of the mechanical philosophy that material bodies as such could not strictly initiate any change in the world, either on other bodies[12] or on minds.[13] It was, however, only later that he denied the possibility of a true (metaphysical) action of minds on bodies. Prior to arriving at his system of pre-established harmony, in 1686, he seems not to have wavered in his belief in the power of minds or incorporeal beings to effect changes in matter. Such a semi-occasionalism is not obviously coherent but, since Leibniz appears not to have confronted the difficulties and in any case moved on to a position for which they did not arise, I shall not elaborate on them.

The other main point of agreement stressed in this 1679 letter concerned the doctrine most of all associated with Malebranche, that we 'see all things in God'. Leibniz liked this phrase and much later in life we find him insisting that a good sense can be given to it. But he never seems to have believed the full-blown Malebranchean doctrine. In the process of drafting the *Discourse* he had first declared that we see all things in God but then later changed the 'in' to 'by'. And that apparently tiny change epitomises the relation between the authentic doctrine of the author of the *Recherche* and the version preferred by Leibniz. What he liked about the doctrine was its commitment to the thought that there is no immediate cause acting on us from outside excepting God alone. It is in virtue of God's mediation and providence that our ideas represent to us anything outside ourselves at all. But seeing all things in God did not mean our very ideas being in God, according to Leibniz. He seems always to have supposed, and in this was to agree with Arnauld, that when we see we must in some sense have ideas of our own.

For a while Leibniz appears to have thought that all things are mirrored in God - God being both the medium through which we see external objects and the light by which we see them. We see these objects through and by means of God because they are reflected in Him. This is the account given in Leibniz's so-called *System of Theology* of the early 1680s. Leibniz claimed, like the author of the *Search after Truth*, that the only way to explain how bodies can act on one another or the soul was to suppose that we see all things in God:

> God is the sole immediate object of the mind outside of itself....it is only through the medium of God our ideas represent to us what passes in the world; for on no other supposition can it be conceived how the body can act on the soul, or how different created substances can act on one another.[15]

In the *Discourse* it is still possible to find traces of this view and of Leibniz's semi-occasionalism. In the draft of # 32, for instance, Leibniz states: 'Only God acts on me...other substances are nothing but occasional causes'. He also wrote: 'One can say that God alone is the immediate object outside for us and that we see all things through him...' (# 28) By this stage, however, Leibniz was no longer supposing one great mirror in which everything that happens is reflected and which, so to say, miraculously and providentially transmits our ideas to us. Instead he developed further a thought that is already expressed in the *System of Theology*, namely, that our mind is itself 'a mirror of God and of the universe'.[16] In the *Discourse* and later writings he extended this thought Neoplatonically to all substances. Every created thing is portrayed as a reflection of the divinity, imitating (so far as it can) both God's omniscience and His omnipotence. It is, moreover, a microcosm of the whole universe, expressing in its full concept or nature everything that happens - not just to itself but in the entire universe.[17]

The *Discourse* marks a turning-point in the development of Leibniz's thought in relation to occasionalism. After the very Malebranchean passages with which the work opens, he hints at one of his main points of departure. He was concerned, in # 8, to distinguish adequately, as he thought Malebranche could not, between the actions of God and the actions of creatures. What troubled Leibniz was that, if God were the only true cause, it seemed to follow that God was also the only true substance. This is the problem Leibniz sought to solve by introducing his much-discussed version of the Scholastic principle of *inesse*. He introduced this principle in the *Discourse* as a statement about the nature of truth, namely, that in all true propositions the concept of the predicate is contained in the concept of its subject. But he went on to interpret this *inesse* relation as implying that everything that is true of a substance is contained in and is deducible from its complete concept. He did not make it immediately clear how he thought this meant that created substances are, after all, true causes with actions of their own distinguishable from those of the Creator. In # 33, however, he makes it clear that it means that 'it follows from the very idea or essence of the soul that all its appearances or perceptions arise spontaneously out of its own nature'.

The thought behind this remark seems to be as Scholastic as its language, except that in the place of autonomous general natures or essences Leibniz has substituted autonomous individual natures or essences. Since everything that happens to a substance is a consequence of its having the nature it has, it is independent from and cannot be acted on by external things. (# 32) Thus it cannot naturally be created or destroyed and could only be created or destroyed by a divine miracle. (# 9)

In articulating his theory of substance Leibniz appears to be assuming that conception of causality according to which a cause contains its effects and according to which statements about those effects can be deduced from statements about the nature of the cause. In short he appears to be falling back on just that view of natural causality with which occasionalism is to be contrasted. But even if this were in itself a step in the right direction it is not a step that could consistently have been taken by the author of the *Discourse on Metaphysics*. For at this stage Leibniz himself was still too much of an occasionalist.

The contrast between the occasionalist and the Scholastic view of Nature is one that the occasionalists themselves were eager to insist upon.[18] According to the Scholastic Aristotelian view, Nature is a realm of autonomous powers that somehow inhere in substances. The religiously orthodox had never been wholly comfortable with the idea

84

of a Nature so independent of the Creator. Moreover, many of the modern philosophers, especially the Cartesians, wanted to reject the 'occult powers' such a view of Nature involved. The occasionalists attacked the Scholastic view on both fronts and in their usage the phrase 'Pagan view of Nature' was a pejorative one.

In his *Traité de la Nature et de la Grâce* of 1680, Malebranche stated his opposition to the Scholastic view in these terms:

> ...The Nature of the Pagan Philosophers is an illusion. What can properly be called 'Nature' is nothing but the general laws that God has established for creating and conserving His Work by the most simple means, by doing what is always orderly, constant [as well as] perfectly worthy of an infinite wisdom and a universal cause.[19]

Leibniz was much impressed by Malebranche's *Treatise* and similar ideas can also be found in his *Discourse* of 1686. His striking remark that Nature is nothing more than 'a custom of God' (# 7) is an expression of a theocentric and occasionalist view of nature. In another work belonging to the *Discourse* period Leibniz went so far as to write: 'What we call *causes* are, in metaphysical rigour, only concomitant requisites'.[20] Nature is regular but there is nothing intrinsically necessary about the usual pattern of events. Within the occasionalist view of Nature put forward in the *Discourse* there is no room for talk of natural necessities and impossibilities.

What I am alluding to is what might be called the 'proto-Humean tendency' of occasionalism - the tendency to reduce causation to constant conjunctions. Leibniz, at least during his *Discourse* period, showed this tendency. He and the occasionalists did not, or course, go as far as Hume. They held a double doctrine of causality. Occasional causes were, so to speak, second-class causes to be contrasted with true causes. So far Leibniz was in agreement with Malebranche. But he wanted to avoid the risk of pantheism implicit in the claim that only God acts, that only God is a 'true cause'. Malebranche in effect retained the necessary connection view for the single case of God - who, as a uniquely omnipotent being could not consistently be supposed to will something without its actually happening.[21] The regularity view applied to everything else. There need be no inconsistency about such a double doctrine of causality if the doctrines apply to different objects, as they do for Malebranche. But in Leibniz's case there is a problem of consistency, since some of the objects to which his two doctrines apply are the same. Material substances, in particular, are assumed in the *Discourse* to be real substances. So at least some of Leibniz's created substances, according to that account, are part of Nature. The *Discourse* thus involves an incoherent account of causation in Nature.

Leibniz's difficulty in distinguishing his position clearly and consistently from that of the occasionalists has, not surprisingly, been a source of confusion for his commentators from his time to our own. One of the commonest confusions is encouraged by his frequent charge that occasionalism required God to perform 'perpetual miracles', to be a *deus ex machina*.[22]   Leibniz's use of the phrase '*deus ex machina*' was a rather esoteric one. He used it, for instance, in a deliberate misquotation from a line of Horace.   The Horace quotation[23] is *Nec Deus intersit, nisi dignus indice nodus inciderit* ('And let no god intervene unless a knot comes worth such a deliverer'). Leibniz seems to have regarded this as a kind of motto for Modern philosophy.   In his *Confession of Nature against the Atheists* he glosses this motto by the words: 'in explaining corporeal phenomena, we must not unnecessarily resort to God or to any other incorporeal thing, form, or quality.'[24]   It is this motto of Modern philosophy, so glossed, that Leibniz invoked against the occasionalists. In his letter to Arnauld of 9 October, 1687, Leibniz suggests that the occasionalists regarded the union of the soul and the body as just such a knot that it was worthy of a *Deus ex machina* to untie.[25] He for his part explained the union of the soul and the body 'in a natural way'. The pseudo-Horatian use by Leibniz of the phrase *Deus ex machina* brings out that the issue is not at all a theological one about what sort of conduct is becoming of God but a question of methodology. It is, in effect, a kind of razor: 'Don't multiply miracles beyond necessity!' So understood, Leibniz's frequently-voiced objection that occasionalists make use of a *Deus ex machina* links closely with his objection in the *Specimen Dynamicum* that the way God is brought into their theory of the union of the soul and the body is 'foreign to the true method of philosophising'.[26]   It is also linked with his point - made in objection to occasionalism - that in philosophy ordinary events should be explained in terms of secondary causes and 'in accordance with the notion of the subject concerned'.[27]

Leibniz seems to have been consistent in his belief that natural philosophy is a secular subject in which scientists should try 'to save or explain natural phenomena (or what is observed in bodies) without taking God as a premise or assuming him in their explanations'.[28]   The appeal to the miraculous has no place in philosophy insofar as it is concerned with the ordinary operations of Nature, in which Leibniz included the communications between substances. The point is not, as many of Leibniz's critics and commentators have supposed,[29] just that it is unworthy of God to tinker and temporise with his creation. Nor is it pertinent to say that Leibniz merely replaces a proliferation of minor miracles with a single grand miracle at the beginning of time. The creation of the world is not a phenomenon in the way that, say, bodily actions are and, for good reason is, not usually thought of as a miracle in any sense.

Nonetheless there is a basis for the popular misconception that Leibniz substituted one grand miracle at the beginning of time for the continuous miracles of the 'way of assistance'. It lies in an analogy Leibniz uses in one of his more superficial but better known explanations of his system of pre-established harmony, one he sent to the editor of the *Histoire des Ouvrages des Savants* in 1696. In this *éclaircissement* to his *New System,* Leibniz uses the analogy of two clocks that are intended to keep in perfect time with one another. Leibniz likens the occasionalists to those who would bring this about by having the clocks supervised by a skilled craftsman constantly setting them right. The best method, however, would be 'to construct the two clocks so skilfully and accurately at the outset that we would be certain of their subsequent agreement'.[30] The suggestion is that it would be unworthy of God to create a universe, as the occasionalists suppose, that required such constant supervision and adjustment.

But, though Leibniz's clock analogy invites this interpretation, it is by no means adequate to explain what he found most objectionable about the reliance upon a *deus ex machina* or upon miracles. Indeed, even in this *éclaircissement*, Leibniz wants to make objections the analogy either does not help or positively obscures. In the first place, he objects that the appeal to miracles is an appeal to something unintelligible – a point that is not captured in the skilled craftsman analogy. He writes that resorting to miracles to explain the communication between mind and body involves making the distinction between them obscure and therefore difficult to believe in.[31] Leibniz was eager, so far as was possible, to make religion as rationally intelligible as possible and was opposed to those to restorted too quickly to faith in matters that could be better understood. Fideism in religious matters was, Leibniz thought, the gateway to scepticism.[32]

In addition to such religious and epistemological objections to a reliance on miracles, Leibniz also wishes, in the *éclaircissement* with the obtrusive two clocks analogy, to make the point about scientific methodology noted earlier. This point is expressed in the complaint against occasionalism: 'this is bringing in the *deus ex machina* for a natural and ordinary thing'.[33] But the nature of this complaint is obscured by its being made in this context, where the *deus ex machina* seems to be a god who is needed to intervene too often. If we look back to the *New System* itself, however, the point is much clearer. In the case of natural and ordinary things, Leibniz wants to say, we should offer explanations in terms of secondary causes. Occasionalism is at fault in abolishing secondary causes and resorting inappropriately to the first cause – the *deus ex machina* – in violation of Leibniz's principle that natural things should be explained by natural causes.

Leibniz only gradually arrived at a clear position about miracles. For some time this was a problematic notion for him, as it was for Malebranche. The criticism that occasionalism required God to perform 'perpetual miracles' implies that miracles may reasonably be supposed to happen sometimes but not all the time. Malebranchean occasionalism, however, does not seem able to allow this and Malebranche at one point went so far as to deny miracles entirely.[34] In that sense of the word in which a miracle is an arbitrary intervention in the order of the world by a fiat of the deity Leibniz was also squarely committed to denying that there are miracles.[35] They were, moreover, both committed to denying that there are miracles in the sense of violations of what is possible in the order of nature. For nothing in nature, according to occasionalism, is strictly impossible. A miracle, as defined in Leibniz's *Discourse* of 1686, is characterised by the fact that it 'could not be foreseen by any created mind, however enlightened'. (# 16) But that account makes it appear that miracles for the author of the *Discourse* are like contingency in Spinoza - a mere appearance due to human ignorance and without any basis in the nature of things.

In these, as in other respects, Leibniz was indebted to his correspondence with Arnauld for enabling him to clarify and develop his views. Arnauld thought that the occasionalists could easily defend themselves against Leibniz's objection that they required God to perform perpetual miracles. Arnauld pointed out that the occasionalists 'do not claim that, every time I want to raise my arm, God brings it about by a new act of will'.[36] On the contrary the raising of any arm was included in the 'single act of the eternal will by which He has chosen to do everything He has foreseen it would be necessary to do.' In Malebranchean terms it required no special miracle but was included within God's 'general will'.

This defence elicited from Leibniz a different definition of 'miracle' from that of the *Discourse*, one that assumes that there are natural modalities, that some things are impossible in the natural course of events. 'God performs a miracle', he wrote to Arnauld, 'when He does anything that surpasses the powers He has given to and conserved in created things'.[37] A miracle, in this sense, is naturally impossible. It surpasses the powers of people to walk on water and so, if they do, that is a miracle. Such stronger conceptions of miracles and natural powers are a feature of Leibniz's later writings. By the turn of the century he could write a paper with the title 'On Nature Itself' with its alternative title 'On the Inherent Force and Actions of Created Things'. Such talk of inherent forces in things would have been foreign to the author of the *Discourse on Metaphysics*.

Leibniz's new-found emphasis on natural powers was further underlined by the controversies in which he became involved in later life. His arguments with the Newtonians, for instance, led him to put more stress on the natural impossibility of gravitation being a property of matter.[38] Another significant case where Leibniz was led to emphasise natural modalities was in his critique of Locke. In the

Preface to the *New Essays*, he opposes Locke's suggestion that God could, if he had so chosen, have endowed matter with the power of thought. He was provoked into saying: '...within the order of nature...it is not at God's arbitrary discretion to attach this or that quality haphazardly to substances'.[39] He does add 'miracles apart' in parenthesis. But since there are no miracles within the order of nature this parenthesis does not serve as a qualification. It seems Leibniz really did want to deny that it is open for God to change the properties of substances. God might, of course, miraculously empower a man to walk on water on a particular occasion or even on many occasions. But that would not be an alteration to human powers. Nor would it be an arbitrary decision since it would be part of the general order God has foreseen from all eternity.

Leibniz was not happy with Locke's suggestion that we might be a peculiar kind of material being, endowed with the power of thought. For then the hope of immortality would rest entirely on faith. And Leibniz thought - shrewdly perhaps - that such a fideistic view of immortality would serve only to promote scepticism. It seemed, therefore, essential to defend the natural immortality of souls. He sought to argue that all true substances, and *a fortiori* souls, were naturally indestructible. And, though more was required for immortality - for instance, memory, the basic point was that substances were essentially the kind of thing that could not be destroyed, i.e. were naturally impervious to the processes of bodily decay and dissolution.

This later tendency to stress an autonomous Nature and the power inherent in created things made Leibniz's system, as later defended, significantly different from the theocentric occasionalism of Malebranche and the author of the *Discourse on Metaphysics*. But, paradoxically, he may have felt closer to Malebranche in his later years. He seems to have become embattled against philosophies that encouraged either no religion or at best what he saw as false religion. His *Theodicy* was written as a corrective to Bayle's Manicheism. And his *New Essays* seem also to have been conceived as a corrective to false religion.[40] In this context it is, I think, significant that it was to Malebranche that he confided what was probably his true opinion of Locke. He wrote in an undated letter that he was trying to combat 'certain lax philosophers, like Locke, le Clerc and their like, who have false and base ideas of man, of the soul, of the understanding and even of the Divinity and who treat everything that goes beyond their popular and superficial notions as illusory'.[41] By contrast with Locke, Leibniz went on to imply, he and Malebranche had two very important attributes in common - a knowledge of the mathematical sciences and an understanding of the nature of eternal truths. Even though they were objectively further apart by this stage, perhaps it seemed to Leibniz that, relative to the tendencies of early eighteenth century philosophy, the gap between his philosophy and Malebranche's was not so wide. It is understandable that he should suggest that 'le passage des Causes occasionnelles à l'Harmonie préétablié ne paroist pas fort difficile'.[42] But the suggestion was nonetheless untrue.

Notes

1. C. I. Gerhardt, ed., *Die Philosophischen Schriften von Gottfried Wilhelm Leibniz*, (Berlin, 1875-90, reprinted Hildesheim: Olms, 1978), 1: 382 (hereafter referred to as *Philosophische Schriften*).

2. *Philosophische Schriften*, 4 : 483.

3. *Philosophische Schriften*, 3 : 625.

4. *Leibnizens Mathematische Schriften*, ed. C. I. Gerhardt, (Berlin: Asher, 1849-55), 2 : 299.

5. Thomas M. Lennon and Paul J. Olscamp, eds. and trans., *Nicolas Malebranche: The Search after Truth*, (Columbus, Ohio State University Press, 1980) (hereafter cited as *Lennon & Olscamp*).

6. This is evident in the early sections of the Discourse on Metaphysics and in some of his critical writings on Descartes. See R. Niall. D. Martin and Stuart Brown, edd. and trans., *G. W. Leibniz: Discourse on Metaphysics and Related Writings*, (Manchester University Press, 1988), 11ff., 103ff. (hereafter cited as *Martin & Brown*).

7. *Martin & Brown*, 115, from A. Robinet, *Malebranche et Leibniz*, (Paris, 1955), 481.

8. *Critique de la Recherche de la vérité*.. (Paris, Coustelier, 1675, reprinted with an Introduction by Richard A. Watson, New York, Johnson Reprint, 1969) (hereafter cited as *Critique*).

9. *Dissertation sur la recherche de la vérité, contenant l'apologie des academiciens....pour servir de Réponse à la Critique de la Critique, etc.....* (Paris, Michallet, 1687).

10. Felix Rabbe, *Étude philosophique, L'abbé Simon Foucher chanoine de la Sainte Chappelle de Dijon*, (Paris, Didier, 1867), Appendix x1ii.

11. *Philosophische Schriften*, 1 : 330.

12. See, for instance, *Philosophische Schriften*, 4: 107. Leibniz inferred from this that 'no body has a principle of motion within itself apart from a concurring mind'. See Deutsche Akademie der Wissenschaften, edd., *G.W.*

Leibniz: Sämtliche Schriften und Briefe, (Darmstadt and Leibzig, 1923--) VI i 509 (hereafter cited as *Sämtliche Schriften*).

13. Leibniz agreed with Malebranche, in an earlier letter of 1679, that it was inconceivable that a substance which had nothing but extension, without thought, could act on a substance which had nothing but thought, without extension. (*Philosophische Schriften* 1 : 327).

14. S 28. See *Martin & Brown*, 72.

15. C.W. Russell, ed., *Leibniz: System of Theology*, (London, Burns & Lambert, 1850), 73.

16. ibid., 73.

17. See, for instance, *Discourse*, # 9.

18. See Charles J. McCracken, *Malebranche and British Philosophy*, (Oxford, Clarendon Press, 1983), Ch. 3.

19. Ginette Dreyfus, ed., *Malebranche: Traité de la Nature et la Grace*, OCM V, 148.

20. Louis Couturat, ed., *Opuscules et fragments inédits de Leibniz*, (Paris, 1903), 521, *Martin and Brown*, 136.

21. See *Lennon & Olscamp*, 448.

22. See, for instance, *Philosophische Schriften*, 1 : 382 (*Brown & Martin*, p. 131), 4 : 483-4.

23. Ars poetica 191 d-.

24. *Philosophische Schriften*, 1: 106.

25. *Philosophische Schriften*, 2: 113.

26. Leroy Loemker ed. *Gottfried Wilhelm Leibniz: Philosophical Papers and Letters*, 2nd edition, Dordrecht, D. Reidel, 1969, p. 445.

27. *Philosophische Schriften*, 4: 484.

28. *Philosophische Schriften*, 4: 105.

29. Richard A. Watson summarises Foucher's critical reaction to Leibniz's system of pre-established harmony as follows:

> This...is nothing more than Malebranchian occasionalism with all the adjustments made at once.
>
> (*Critique*, xxvi.)

If that were a correct account Leibniz would also be exposed to the charge of having been unfair to Malebranche, a charge made by Morris Ginsberg:

> The theory of occasionalism as worked out by him [Malebranche] does not imply, as Leibniz so frequently urged, and is sometimes maintained now, a series of miracles at every moment, for God, according to Malebranche, acts in accordance with general volitions, i.e. general laws. The adaptation of movement to ideas, for example, is the result of the laws of the communication of motion and the laws of the conjunction of body and soul, and God, having once laid down these laws, the rest follows as a matter of strict necessity. Thus interpreted, the theory of occasionalism comes very near to Leibniz's own doctrine of pre-established harmony.

(Morris Ginsberg, trans., *Dialogues on Metaphysics and on Religion by Nicolas Malebranche*, London, Allen & Unwin, 1923, 63((hereafter referred to as *Ginsberg*).

30 *Philosophische Schriften*, 4: 499.

31. "...so long as it was necessary to explain the communication of mind and body by a kind of miracle, it remained open for some people to fear that the distinction between them might not be what it was supposed to be, because defenders of the distinction had to go to such lengths to uphold it..." (*Philosophische Schriften*, 4 : 500).

32. I have discussed this aspect of Leibniz's thought further in "Christian Averroism, fideism and the 'two-fold truth'", in *The Philosophy in Christianity*, ed. Godfrey Vesey, *Supplement to Philosophy* 1990.

33. *Philosophische Schriften*, 4 : 499

34. 'Dieu ne fait jamais de miracles, il n'agit jamais pas des volontez particulieres contre ses propres loix, que l'Ordre ne le demande ou ne le permette'. (*Entretiens sur la Métaphysique*, OCM XII 95, *Ginsberg*, 129.)

35. See *Discourse*, # 7.

36.   *Philosophische Schriften*, 2 : 84.

37.   *Philosophische Schriften*, 2 : 93.

38.   This became a pre-occupation of the last years of Leibniz's life and is
      reflected in a number of writings, particularly in the Clarke Correspondence
      and in Leibniz's polemical *Anti-barbarus physicus* (*Philosophische
      Schriften*, 7: 337-44, esp. 338-9, trans. Roger Ariew and Daniel Garber edd.
      G.W. Leibniz: Philosophical Essays, Indianopolis, Hackett, 1989, 312ff.,
      esp. 314.)

39.   *Sämtliche Schriften*, VI : 6: 66.

40.   See Nicholas Jolley, *Leibniz and Locke*, (Oxford, Clarendon Press, 1984).

41.   *Philosophische Schriften*, 7 : 361.

42.   *Philosophische Schriften*, 3: 625.

7   Malebranche and Locke: The Theory of Moral Choice, a Neglected Theme

JEAN MICHEL VIENNE

TRANS. R. N. D. MARTIN

Seeing ideas in God and the consequences of that for the nature of ideas are two of the theses on which Malebranche and Locke are opposed. Many commentators have analysed these divergences,[1] but they must not mask the convergences likewise present: both have a 'representative theory of ideas', and they equally agree that the (simple) idea is passively received,[2] that it cannot be innate[3], nor produced by the (supposedly scholastic) volatile species[4], or by generalizing abstraction. It is to be regretted that the Locke text usually relied on for comparing the two writers takes no account of the numerous similarities, and its level is mainly that of a boring and repetitive refutation of theses whose internal coherence is not grasped at all. How then could a serious comparison between the two authors be conducted on such bases and how also could we explain the great importance Malebranche had in Locke's eyes: a decade before the *Examination of P. Malebranche's Opinion*[5] Locke stated that Malebranche had written 'many fine things, which have rightly contributed to his reputation in the world', adding that 'so great, so penetrating a mind can be corrected for having asserted some unreasonable things.'[6] It is certain that the difference between the assessments of 1684 and those of 1693 (date of the drafting of the

94

notes on Malebranche and the vision in God[7]) can be explained by the development of Malebranche's and Locke's theses: first, many controversies had followed the publication of Malebranche's writings, and Locke was in the Netherlands with a ringside seat; second, Locke's note is in fact a quotation from Arnauld's critique, *Des Vrayes et des Fausses Idées*, published about a year and a half earlier; third, the debate with Norris, who presented himself as Malebranche's disciple, also had its effects. It remains that in 1695, Locke retains a 'personal kindness' towards him though he may have written some altogether unintelligible things,[8] and that, as will be seen, many of his reflexions rest on analyses of Malebranche. How can such contradictory assessments be explained? Above all, can a comparison between these two writers who seem separated in everything contribute something to an understanding of both?

The thesis defended here is addressed to these questions. Locke and Malebranche read each other at different levels. Malebranche's psychology of error and psychology of moral choice are the core of what Locke admired and continued to admire, but this psychological level, however, rests on a 'metaphysics' that Locke cannot accept: the more he follows Malebranche, by adapting him, in his psychological descriptions, the more Locke rejects the 'metaphysical' background that supplies their rationale, and *vice versa*. In this context, the idea is the *instrument* forming, in Locke as in Malebranche, the link between these two levels, so much so that it is on the idea that the oppositions harden, all the more bitter because they arise out of a disappointment. The idea is the most visible and fragile link in the chain uniting the two levels, and Malebranche criticizes Locke because he reduces the idea to perception, while Locke rejects the intellectual intuition that Malebranche grants himself too freely. The fundamental question raised by the idea is then the connection between experience and its 'metaphysical' background, its possibility, and its mechanism.

I need only two witnesses. The first is indirect, just a note from Locke's reading, copied from Malebranche's regular adversary, Arnauld:

> It is not only the ambiguity of the word idea that creates much confusion in the work of this author, but it is a widespread fault in his *Treatise on Nature and Grace*, where different meanings of similar words seem to give rise to great mysteries that will disappear as soon as the equivocations have been sorted out.[9]

Locke agrees with Arnauld in criticizing the excessively loose 'analogy' lying behind not only the thesis of the vision in God but the whole of his thought: other terms in Malebranche have a transcendent sense instituting a 'mysterious' metaphysic that is out of place. At that point, Malebranche's criticism is illuminating, for it makes exactly the opposite objection to Locke: not of taking analogy too far, but on the contrary of reducing the idea to its sensible dimension alone, which comes back to the downgrading of all science and all morality:

> If ideas cannot be distinguished from perceptions... (we fall back into the positions of Hobbes and Locke)... and there will not any more be either true nor false, immutably so, neither just nor unjust, neither science nor morality.[10]

The criticism is completely parallel to that made by Lowde, by Leibniz, and by Lady Masham herself[11]: science and morality (the first is conceived as the basis for the other) fall into the contingent, the relative and the conventional, if there is no intellectual intuition of either the one genus or the other [innateness, moral sense]. Just here is the centre of the debate between the two writers, a debate of which the nature of ideas is no more than a symptom: morality falls into either conventionalism, or into intolerance, according as the idea is conceived as an individual psychological state or as the clear perception of the divine thinking.

It must not be forgotten that Locke's criticism of Malebranche derives from the fact that he sees in him a new manifestation of that *enthusiasm* he has been fighting since he grasped the dangers caused to peace by all 'spontaneist' sects. It is just when drafting the supplementary chapter on *enthusiasm* for the fourth edition of the *Essay*, that Locke starts again on an (almost complete) reading of the *Recherche*, and it is from within a criticism of the claimed immediateness of vision of the *enthusiasts* that he denounces the 'vanity, inconsistency and unintelligibility of that way of explaining human understanding'.[12] Molyneux confirms this: 'He is mostly Platonick, and in some things almost enthusiastical'[13]. When we reread from this angle the posthumous manuscripts explicitly devoted to Malebranche or Norris we understand that for Locke, disparaging secondary causes and introducing intelligible (i.e. abstract) ideas are not without consequences for the moral, religious and political life, and that it is for this reason that he opposes Malebranche.

While Locke condemns the enthusiastical use of an analogical vocabulary, he follows Malebranche in its immanent use: in his eyes the idea ought to be reduced to its sensible aspect, and separated from the whole metaphysical apparatus encumbering it. Even more than in relation to the idea, it is interesting to analyse this difference in relation to feeling. In what follows I shall confine myself to that 'moral psychology' that much preoccupied both writers because of its religious implications (sin, predestination and grace), which in the eyes of the thinkers of the time were more important than the 'theory of representation'.[14] The analysis could be pursued with equal fertility in relation to the psychology of error and the reform of the understanding.

Let us begin by comparing their definitions of the Good. For Malebranche:

> Every pleasure is a good and actually makes happy him who enjoys it at the moment he enjoys it, and to the extent that he enjoys it, and every pain is an evil that actually makes unhappy him who suffers it at the moment that he suffers it and to the extent that he suffers it.[15]

While Locke, for his part, asserts:

> First, that which is properly good or bad, is nothing but barely Pleasure or Pain... As to present Pleasure and Pain, the Mind ... never mistakes that which is really good or evil; that which is the greater Pleasure, or the greater Pain, is really just as it appears.[15]

The two texts are parallel, and if it is understandable that the 'empiricist' Locke will define good by pleasure received, it is astonishing to find the Cartesian Malebranche in agreement. Contrariwise, if in other ways we can understand the admiration of Locke for this thinker in whose footsteps his own analysis is going to follow, we will equally understand the virulence of the reaction of the 'rationalists' on the continent against Malebranche's 'betrayal'. A long controversy will follow the publication of the *Traité de la Nature et de la Grâce*, a controversy in which the main participants will be Bayle and Arnauld, the first defending the theses of Malebranche, but from a perspective almost as sceptical and empiricist as Locke's, the second defending the necessity and *a priori* character of the Good and displeased at seeing them thus put at risk by a Father of the Oratory.[17] Malebranche, Arnauld, Bayle, an intellectual microcosm Locke knows and reads, and may perhaps have frequented.

Identical definitions of the Good by pleasure, identical pretensions too to rationalize the conversion from limited and temporary goods to the supreme and eternal Good. But it is in the way this process is rationalized that the divergences reappear. For, Malebranche, the pleasure of the moment counts for nothing without participation in the supreme Good, and the individual must pass from the effect to the cause, from the appearance to the reality, from the popular and physical sense to the true and spiritual sense of the word good. This is the joint task of the will (love examines what it loves) and of the understanding[18]. For Locke, on the other hand, between finite pleasure and the supreme Good there is no relation of participation, only a purely quantitative relation, and man must learn to pass from the one to the other, by the intellectual discovery of the need to enlarge his temporal horizon. For Malebranche, pleasure is the appearance of a spiritual reality, a reality to be discovered by a qualitative jump; for Locke, pleasure is a reality which appears as such, the initial stage of a movement which will enlarge the durations from stage to stage.

To mark clearly the scope of the this resemblance in difference, let us consider for a moment Malebranche's thesis on its own[19]. The will is distinct from the understanding, particularly in the way it receives impressions of motions and inclinations; it is essentially passive. At the same time, however, considered from God's point of view, the will is the love of the Good in general (and hence of God) which it cannot help aiming at. In this sense, the will does not possess the freedom of indifference. Because this aim is at the good in general, this particular act of volition is necessary to determine it to this particular good.[20] the first question then arising is to know whether the particular volition is good in that it actualizes (effects) the general will, or whether it is evil, in that it turns the will away from its ultimate goal, which is also God himself.[21] Hence a second question: to what extent is the good in general an abstract essence present in all the particular goods, and to what extent is it a personal good, God himself? These are the traditional questions of neo-Platonic ethics.

Besides the will, there is desire, which seems to be a volition considered at the level of occasional causes and no longer at the level of efficient causes as above.[22] The desire, as a will applied to a particular good, permits the pleasure of satisfaction, which it seeks in seeking for this or that good. It's at this level that the identity of volition, pleasure and the good is fully justified. The 'empiricist' or 'utilitarian' analysis of Malebranche is then only the 'human' point of view on an operative reality, different in nature. The first analysis is possible for Malebranche only because another reality gives it meaning.

But the gap between the two levels, empirical and metaphysical, is far from secondary: it has a function in the interplay of forces constituting the moral psychology of the individual. In the gap between the will as divine power in us aiming at the perfectly good and the volition as a desire for this or that finite good, there is a remainder, the motor of concrete moral life, and a sort of unused force maintaining a permanent tension and expressed by the word *inquiétude*[23] (anxiety). *Inquiétude* can be considered in relation to each of its 'progenitors': either, as the fruit of an infinite will, *inquiétude* is a perpetual motion and inability to stay still[24]; or as the human finitude of desire, it is impossibility for a limited good to satisfy the soul.[25]

Inquiétude is the cause of *suspens*,[26] a notion no more new than that of *inquiétude*, but the application to moral psychology of the general attitude proposed by Pyrrho (and Descartes) seems specifically Malebranchian. The power to suspend judgement is the "principle" of freedom, in that it realizes 'the invincibility of the will with respect to this or that particular good'.[27] Like *inquiétude*, it is the fruit of the will itself, the only operative cause, and not of the understanding, which remains a power of truth and light, while the will concerns feeling.[28]

This brief reminder of some elements of Malebranche's moral psychology allows us to underline what is essential for his relation to Locke: the analysis of the will from two different points of view (metaphysical and psychological) permits the simultaneous coexistence of a tendency towards the supreme God and a "realist" description of choice, to derive the essential element of empirical choice, *inquiétude*. The empirical description has no coherence apart from the appeal to the metaphysical background or, to put the same point differently, liberated by its background from every apologetic preoccupation, the psychological description can be realistic.

If we compare the description just given of moral psychology in Malebranche's terms with the attentive examination Locke made of it in Book II, Chapter 21 of his *Essay*, we are led to think that the first draft, like the corrections made in the second edition, are the fruit of an interpretative reading by Locke of Malebranche's theses. We know already that one of the corrections (we shall see that it is fundamental) of the second edition was made because Locke 'was aiming at Fr. Malebranche here'.[29] Apart from this biographical aspect, the question is: "Under what structural constraints, and in what ways, does Locke rewrite the moral psychology he has read in Malebranche, and in view of what insufficiencies does he consider he has to correct his first interpretation the second time round?"

The first point is the distinction between the will and the understanding. For the more nominalistic Locke only individuals exist. In the first edition, he draws a first, still limited, conclusion from this partial nominalism: will and understanding are so far distinct (it would be absurd, as Malebranche agrees, to imitate the scholastics by confusing these two powers[30]) that a person cannot be obliged to believe what is evident (thereby justifying tolerance). In general, the true, the object of the understanding, and the good, the object of the will, have nothing in common, and the true can neither arouse nor motivate the will.[31] Nevertheless, in the first edition, Locke in practice contradicts his demand for the separation of the two faculties: the will remains a power with an intellectual component, since it aims at, and in that measure, discerns the supreme Good (which is absent) and is determined by it. Just like Malebranche, then, and as with him, human perfection and the greatest liberty fundamentally reside in ordering to the supreme Good through the choices of derived goods.[32]

The whole question is then to know what this supreme Good is. Is it the supreme Good *per se* (possibly God), or the supreme good for the subject? The will, for sure, is always determined by the *appearance* of the supreme Good - Bayle and Arnauld had been in controversy over this theme in 1686.[33] The question was to know whether the subjectively perceived good had a relation to the objectively supreme Good. Locke, - unsurprisingly, since he was in the Netherlands at the time of the controversy, and was then starting work on the *Essay* - put the question in Chapter 21 of his second book, basing his analysis on the expression *appearance*.[34] He sets out from the subjective plane: pleasure and good are not distinct - in the eyes of him who experiences the pleasure - for in matters of feeling apparent and real are one single identical thing. With him the apparent is neither illusory nor a substitute, but the manifest: 'The apparent and the real are, in this case, always identical'.

Locke places himself, in other respects and in a subsidiary way, on the level of the divine: like each of the protagonists in the debate, he agrees to retain the objective distinction between earthly goods and the Good. But the difficulties Malebranche already met increase with Locke: how to justify on the basis of the subjective criterion of pleasure the objective necessity to turn towards a higher good, difficulties all the more severe because in this first edition, Locke had come to use the expression "supreme Good" to designate the subjectively felt good. If the good we enjoy is the supreme Good (this is subjectively true since the felt experience instantaneously occupies the entire mind), there is no longer any tension to come and call the subject out of it to experience a good considered objectively greater. There is no longer anything to explain how the individual frees himself in practice from the good that is for him the supreme Good to submit himself to the will of "God, the righteous judge",[35] unless by a clairvoyance - inexplicable - of absent goods not spoiled by pain. Locke lacks, for example, the tension of *inquiétude* introduced by Malebranche through the difference between will and desire.

On top of this first difficulty, there is another, wrongly imputed to Malebranche by Arnauld, but fully applicable against Locke: how can we say that we are free and moral when the Supreme Good we believe we are aiming at is objectively no more than a particular good?[36]

These difficulties affect not only the theory of choice, but also, and above all, the definition of morality and liberty, and I propose to see in them the reason pushing Locke to alter his text for the second edition. He himself recognizes that while in his first version he sought to speak only of the will, he was led despite himself to move from the question of choice to that of liberty, a question with redoubtable consequences, such as that of predestination[37] (which he does not want to treat). Here we are right at the centre of the debates of the time, between divine science and the ordering of the human will by the divine, as seen by a Protestant with Arminian tendencies reacting against the Puritanism dominant around him.

The solution adopted in Locke's second edition is radical: to suppress all reference to the supreme Good,[38] a move understandable as the rejection of the last residue of essentialism: no particular good participates in any way in the supreme Good, but each counts on its own. The solution is perfectly coherent with the identity of pleasure with the good. A new delimitation differentiates this particular good from the greater Good: duration. As often with Locke, an empirical difference between the good of the moment and the eternal good replaces the conceptual or metaphysical difference, and the calculus of durations replaces the intuition of the good *per se*.[39]

This change entailed others, which, curiously, will use against Malebranche (or what Locke reads from Malebranche) elements of the Malbranchian theory Locke had neglected in his first version. Hence the second edition will give a fundamental rôle to three notions, notions, as we have seen, important for Malebranche: desire, *inquiétude* and *suspens*. So much so that the description of choice will become, for different reasons, closer to that of Malebranche.

Desire replaces the appetitive aspect of the will. Of the will, properly so-called there remains no more than the executor of the final resolution, mere machinery permitting the choice to be put into effect. Desire on the other hand becomes the power 'in tension towards'. There is nothing surprising about this rereading of Malebranche, as soon as the aim at the supreme Good is removed.[40] Nothing surprising, then about Locke's illusion, passed on by Coste, according to which Locke was only sorting out Malebranche's confusions. It is this desire that in Locke constantly retains energy beyond this or that choice:[41] a human power (in all likelihood preordained by the Creator) replaces what in Malebranche was the gap between "metaphysical" will and human volition. The possibility of conversion thus remains open without an appeal to an intuition of the supreme Good; there is no grasp, not even at the level of feeling, of the Good *per se*. The practical intuition of the Good is rejected in favour of a blind tendency receiving the name innate refused to the idea.

Malebranche's *inquiétude* has its parallel in Locke's *uneasiness*. As far as we can understand a text in which Locke is far from clear, the terms *inquiétude* and *uneasiness* are not synonyms, as yet again the French translator remarks, in the knowledge that he is addressing readers acquainted with Malebranche's vocabulary.[42] Uneasiness is purely negative, pure lack, while Malebranchian *inquiétude* aims positively at the supreme Good through the incompleteness of the particular good. Again, uneasiness is a state of mind of the individual, while *inquiétude* additionally designates what is lacking. Uneasiness is dissastifaction without intentionality, but opening the desire to a precise intentional search.[43] It is here that Locke's reduction of the different levels in Malebranche to one alone shows most clearly: instead of being, like *inquiétude*, the remainder of the gap between subjective and objective good, far from being an awareness of the transcendent, uneasiness is a constant state of the character, independent of the good possessed.

Intended to make the connection between desire and uneasiness, suspense is the third point introduced into the second edition of the *Essay* which raises the suspicion of a borrowing from Malebranche's conceptualization. It is thanks to suspense that the understanding can guide desire, which unlike Malebranche's will, no longer has either an orientation towards the Good, nor a capacity to examine what it loves. In Malebranche, suspense had the function of providing a speculative assurance of an orientation towards the Good already in essentials realized in the will. In Locke, suspense has the function of introducing the orientation towards the supreme Good *de novo*: thanks to suspense, the understanding, the only faculty able, by its calculations, to discover the supreme Good (i.e. the most durable good), can intervene for the first time. Thanks to suspense, the understanding comes to order to the most durable good a desire that has no privileged relation with it. The immediate and essential orientation in Malebranche is replaced in Locke by the opening of a parenthesis in favour of the understanding, the sole power enjoying the divine guarantee. Freedom (and human dignity) depend no longer on the fixation of the will on the supreme Good, but on the intervention of the "divine light in man" considering and examining.[44] Freedom is no longer the exploitation of the superabundance of the will going as far as examining intellectually the nature of what it loves and is disappointed by: on the contrary freedom is in the breaking up of the empire of affectivity in favour of a completely foreign power. Thus in Locke the understanding alone seems to lie behind the suspense which opens for itself a space, and the understanding alone is the condition for salvation.

It would be worthwhile to carry further the detailed comparison of the vocabulary and thought of our two authors on the psychology of error. But the sample we have examined suffices to show the interest in the parallel and to establish a strong presumption in favour of the thesis according to which Locke wrote this chapter having in mind the Malebranchian thesis and the controversy issuing from it. Even if, historically, we have no certainty on this matter, the comparison is effective enough theoretically: it allows us to delimit better just what constitutes the two systems of thought.

At the outset, the "empiricism" of Malebranche which irritated Arnauld and rejoiced Bayle has meaning only through the link to a "metaphysical" theory of the will. Locke does not accept this "metaphysical" dimension, which to his eyes depends on undue "analogy" - indeed on a play upon words - any more than he accepts the vision in God thesis, and for the same reason. The slip in the first edition of the *Essay* makes even more manifest his concern to avoid every trace of an intellectual intuition of a world of the *per se*. His fear of *enthusiasm* makes him agree with Arnauld in limiting the capacities of human understanding, but since no revelation can obtain simple ideas, man is reduced to constructing them from sensible experience, since the "absent" idea of salvation is beyond the limits of the moment. Since, moreover, he rejects Bayle's fideism just as much as Malebranche's occasionalism, he cannot be sure that empirical moral psychology opens out on to a divine plan for man's salvation.

Hence, though he agrees with Malebranche's psychological observations, Locke has to ensure their link with salvation in other ways. As always in thought with a nominalistic tendency, it is by an external link that the essential relation is replaced: the understanding calculates the greatest happiness, instead of climbing up the chain of goods to the supreme Good, the effective cause of secondary goods.

But by this way of linking psychology and salvation, Locke runs into at least three difficulties concerning just those points he has tried to correct in Malebranche. The first concerns the place given to the understanding: all sin is an error, since the understanding alone is at the origin of suspense and of the consideration of the good that desire will choose to make the will execute. As his friend Molyneux remarks, in this conception 'all sins proceed from our understandings, and not from the depravity of our wills',[45] which is inconsistent with some of Locke's assertions, particularly in his religious writings.

The second difficulty lies in the relation of understanding to will. The will is reduced to a pure executive force, empty of all rationality: it follows on from the intervention of the understanding, which itself follows on from uneasiness. Moral psychology is thus reduced to a bare succession of acts whose relations are at a quasi-mechanical level. What Malebranche follows the scholastics in distinguishing *de ratione*, Locke separates *de re*, as if real entities were in question. This is inconsistent with his "nominalism", according to which only individuals, not powers are held to exist, not to mention the fact that he finishes up with an analysis too elementary by far, unable to give an account of the reality of choice, something he will acknowledge under the fire of the criticisms of another friend, Van Limborch.

The third difficulty lies in the fundamental criticism of Malebranche's "enthusiasm". Locke refers to the calculating understanding alone the ability to determine the supreme Good, or, in some texts, the mere exercise (even if ineffective) of the understanding suffices to justify the man who seeks salvation. Hence moral formalism (before Kant) and the salvific activity of the understanding replace the Malebranchian teleology of the will. Even if the understanding has no intuition of eternal truths, as Locke insists in the *Examination*,[46] he is sure of success (on condition he acts "comme il faut"). Thus the teleology of the exercise of the understanding has replaced that of its content (aimed at by the will or the understanding). Locke's difficulty can even be considered greater than that of Malebranche, for, while Malebranche examines the coherence of his teleological conception, Locke accepts without examination the self-styled divine guarantee granted to the right usage of the understanding. The Catholic Malebranche believes that the human will participates in the order and will of God, while the Reformed Locke believes that reasoning is a work meriting justification by God's arbitrary decision.

The astonishing parallelism between the psychological analysis of Locke and Malebranche rests, then, as I have attempted to show above, on different metaphysical and gnoseological positions. But the very difficulties Locke runs into testify to the necessity for him of reintroducing "metaphysical" presuppositions to defend his supposed empiricism. They also testify to the impossibility for an empiricist of avoiding a basis of "metaphysical" positions.

Notes

1. Richard Acworth, *The Philosophy of John Norris of Bemerton, 1657-1712*, Hildesheim, Olms, 1973; François Duchesneau, *L'Empirisme de Locke*, The Hague, Nijoff, 1973; C. S. Johnston, 'Locke's Examination of Malebranche and John Norris', *Journal of the History of Ideas*, 19 (1958) 551-8; C. J. McCracken, *Malebranche and British Philosophy*, Oxford, Clarendon Press, 1983; H. E. Matthews, 'Locke, Malebranche and the representative theory', *The Locke Newsletter* 2, (1971) 12-21; J. Pucelle, edition and introduction to *Locke: Examen de la Vision en Dieu de Malebranche*, Paris, Vrin, 1978; J. Yolton, *Perceptual Acquaintance*, Oxford, Basil Blackwell, 1984 (chapters II and V).

2. *Recherche de la Vérité*, 3.2.3, in N. Malebranche, *Oeuvres Complètes*, 20 vols, Paris, Vrin-CNRS, 1958-66, vol. III, and *Essay concerning Humane Understanding*, 2.2, 2.3. Locke's *Essay* is cited from Nidditch's edition, Oxford at the Clarendon Press, 1975, and his correspondence from the edition of De Beer, Oxford at the Clarendon Press, 1976-89.

3. *Recherche*, 3.2.4 and *Essay*, 1.4.1 and 19.

4. *Recherche*, 3.2.2 and *Essay*, 1.1.8. and 2.8.7.

5. J. Locke, "Examination of Fr. Malebranche's opinion of our *seeing all things in God*", in *Posthumous Works*, 1706. (Written in 1693).

6. Journal, 9 and 15 March 1684, Bodleian Library MS f.8-9. Quotation from A. Arnauld, *Des Vrayes et des Fausses Idées*, Cologne, 1683 (reprinted Paris, Fayard, 1986, p. 160).

7. Letter to Molyneux, 26 April 1695; *Correspondence*, no. 1887.

8.   Molyneux's opinion, letter to Locke of 26 March 1695, *ibid.*, no. 1867, ratified by Locke (letter of 26 April 1695 *ibid.*, no. 1887).

9.   *Journal*, citation from Arnauld, *Des Vrayes et des Fausses Idées*, *op. cit.* (note 6) chapter 21, p. 188.

10.   Letter from Malebranche to Fénelon, June 1713, in *Oeuvres Complètes*, (note 2) XIX, p. 842. Cf. letter from Leibniz to Malebranche, December 1711, *ibid.*, p. 816 and *Recherche*, Éclaircissement X, pp. 132-140; *Réponse au livre des Vrayes et des Fausses Idées*, *Oeuvres Complètes*, VI, p. 23.

11.   Letter to Lady Masham, 7 April, 1688, *Correspondence*, no. 1040.

12.   Letter of 8 March 1694, *ibid.*, no. 1857, cf no, 1620.

13.   Letter of 26 March 1695, *ibid.*, no. 1867, cf nos. 1887, and 2645. This charge had been raised against him by Arnauld and accepted by Malebranche himself: "I prefer being called a visionary, being accused of being an enthusiast...than to agree that bodies might enlighten me..." (*Recherche*, Éclaircissement X, 3, p. 128).

14.   On the relation between the *Recherche* and the *Traité de la Nature et de la Grâce* see the "Introduction" of G. Dreyfus to her edition of the latter (Paris, Vrin, 1958, pp. 53-58. As far as I know the relation between Malebranche and Locke on this point has never been analysed, though there are hints in F. Alquié, *Le Cartésianisme de Malebranche*, Paris, Vrin, 1974, and in Jean Deprun, *La Philosophie de l'Inquiétude en France au XVIIIe siècle*. Paris, Vrin, 1979.

15.   *Recherche*, 4.10.1.

16.   *Essay*, 2.21.61 and 63.

17.   On this controversy, to which my attention was drawn by Jean-Luc Solère, the following may be mentioned:

      A. Arnauld, *Réflexions philosophiques et théologiques sur le Nouveau Système de la Nature et de la Grâce*, Cologne (false address), 1685. See especially chapters 21-24.

      P. Bayle, review of the above, *Nouvelles de la République des Lettres*, Rotterdam, August 1685, Art. III, pp. 860 ff.

      A. Arnauld, *Avis à l'auteur des Nouvelles de la République des Lettres*, Delft (false address), 1685.

P. Bayle, *Réponse de l'auteur des Nouvelles de la République des Lettres à l'Avis...*, Rotterdam, 1686.

A. Arnauld, *Dissertation sur le prétendu bonheur des plaisirs des sens, pour servir de réplique ...*, Cologne (false address), 1687.

N. Malebranche, *Réponse au P. Régis*, Paris, 1693, III, OCM (note 2) XVII-I, pp. 311-18.

A. Arnauld, *3e Lettre à Malebranche*, 1694.

N. Malebranche, *Réponse à la 3e Lettre de M. Arnauld sur les Idées et les Plaisirs ...*, Amsterdam, 1699, *OCM* (note 2), VIII-IX, pp. 976-89.

Cf. See A. Robinet, "Introduction", OCM (note 2) VI, pp. XXII-XXVII.

18.   Cf. *Traité de la Nature et de la Grâce*, 3.4: "The word good is ambiguous: it can mean either the pleasure that makes one formally happy, or the cause of this pleasure, true, or apparent." The true cause is of course God, to whom the name Good properly belongs, even if usage has consecrated the use of the word for the occasional causes or effects, i.e. the feelings felt on the occasion of objects. Cf Letter 3 of 19 March 1699: "Considered in themselves, they are physically true pleasures ... They are produced by the true God as consequences of the wise laws of the union of the Soul and the Body".

19.   On this subject see, notably, F. Alquié, *op. cit.*, (note 14) pp. 325-95, G. Dreyfus, *La Volonté selon Malebranche*, Paris, Vrin, 1958; M. Gueroult, *Malebranche*, Paris, Aubier, 1955, t. III, p. 147-316; J. Laporte, "La Liberté chez Malebranche", *Études d'Histoire de la Philosophie Française au XVII siècle*, Paris, Vrin, 1951.

20.   *Traité de la Nature et de la Grâce*, 3.3.

21.   *Ibid.*, 3.3 and 3.5, *Recherche*, 1.1.2, 4.1.3 and 4.2.2, Éclaircissement I. On the level of moral psychology, the point is the counterpart of the problematic relation between *étendue intelligible* and a particular body.

22.   *Traité de la Nature et de la Grâce*, 2.32.37 and 3.7.

23.   Cf. Deprun, *op. cit.*, (note 14).

24.   *Recherche*, 4.2.1 and 4.2.5 (p. 26).

25.   *Recherche*, 4.2.2; *Traité de la Nature et de la Grâce*, 3.6 and 3.16.

26. *Traité de la Nature et de la Grâce*, 3.6 and 3.16.

27. *Ibid.*, 3.12-13.

28. *ibid .*, 3.32.

29. Note to *Essay*, 2.21.30 (Coste translation, reprint ed. Naert, Paris, Vrin, 1972) on the confusion, to be discussed below, between desire and will.

30. *Essay*, 2.21.17.

31. *Essay*, 1.3.12.

32. *Essay*, 2.21.29-38 in the numbering of the first edition (given by Nidditch in notes to his edition, *op. cit.*, note 2).

33. See for example P. Bayle, *Réponse* (note 17) pp. 21-29. See also the dispute about Quietism between Malebranche and Lamy, *Oeuvres* (note 2) XIV, pp. 7-190.

34. *Essay*, 2.21.7 (first edition): 'Things in their present enjoyment, are what they seem: the apparent and real good, are, in this case, always, the same'. This "subjectivism" is related to Descartes' analysis of the "formal reality of thought". Cf. *Les Passions de l'Ame*, # 26.

35. On this issue consider the join between the second version and the first at 2.21.60 (first edition numbering).

36. Arnauld, *Réflexions*, (note 17) 1.24, III. 2-4, pp. 471-475.

37. Letter to Molyneux of 20 January 1693, *Correspondence,* no. 1592. On the use of time in ethics by Malebranche himself see *Entretiens*, Préface, *Oeuvres* (note 2) XII, p. 7.

38. See e.g. the rewriting of 2.21.29 (first edition) into 2.21.41-42 (second edition).

39. Exactly the opposite move to that in Plato, *Protagoras* 356a-357e.

40. *Essay*, 2.21.30, (Coste translation) (note 29). We can understand that in Locke's eyes Malebranche confuses will and desire, since he makes them the two sides of one single reality, while Locke makes them two purely human capacities, following each other to bring a choice into effect. Cf. the same kind of criticism by Arnauld, *Vrayes et fausses Idées op. cit.*, (note 6), chapter 27, p. 255.

41.   *Essays*, 2.21.62.

42.   Notes to Coste translation (note 29) at 2.20.6 (p. 177) and 2.21.30 (p. 193).

43.   Cf. the reflexion on the intentionality of desire and dissatisfaction, in Arnauld, *Dissertation* (note 17), pp. 121-2.

44.   *Essay*, 2.21.47, 53 and 67.

45.   Letter from Molyneux of 22 December 1692, *Correspondence* no. 1579, cf. MS f.2, f1.42, and *Reasonableness of Christianity*, # 1, *Works* , *London 1759, II, p. 511.*

46.   *Examination*, (note 5) # 52.

8 Malebranche, Arnauld and Berkeley on the Imperceptibility of Outer Objects

GODFREY VESEY

At the beginning of Book 3, Part 2, Chapter 1 of *The Search after Truth* (1674-5) Malebranche wrote:

> I suppose that every one will grant, that we perceive not the Objects that are without us immediately, and of themselves. We see the *Sun*, the *Stars*, and infinite other Objects without us; and it is not probable that the Soul goes out of the Body, and fetches a walk, as I may say, about the Heavens to contemplate all the Objects therein.

> It sees them not therefore by themselves, and the immediate Object of the Mind, when it beholds the *Sun*, for example, is not the *Sun*, but something intimately united to the Soul: and that same thing is what I call our *Idea*. So that by the Term *Idea*, I mean nothing but that Object which is immediate, or next to the Soul in its Perception of any thing.

> It ought to be well observed, that in order to the Mind's perceiving any Object, it is absolutely necessary the Idea of that Object be actually present to it: which is so certain as not possibly to be doubted of. But it is not necessary there should be anything without like to that Idea: for it often happens that we perceive things which don't exist, and which never were in Nature. And so a Man has frequently in his Mind real Ideas of things that never were. When a Man, for instance, imagines a golden Mountain, it is indispensably necessary the Idea of that Mountain should be really present to his Mind.[1]

Commenting on this argument, Antoine Arnauld, in *Des Vraies et des Fausses Idées*, 1683, Ch. 8, distinguished between two senses of 'presence'. There is spatial presence and there is objective presence. Two objects are spatially present to one another if there is not a significant distance between them. For there to be objective presence one of the terms must be a mind: an object's objective presence to a mind is the mind thinking of, or perceiving, the object. Something can be objectively present to someone and yet spatially distant from him, or even non-existent - like a golden mountain.

Arnauld says that overlooking the distinction between spatial and objective presence means that people attach two very erroneous meanings to the proposition, 'Bodies must be present to the soul for it to be acquainted with them.' He writes:

> The first erroneous meaning is that people have imagined the *presence* to be a prerequistite of the soul's acquaintance with the bodies, and that it is necessary, so that the bodies are in a position to be known; whereas the presence of the object in our mind, being none other than an *objective presence*, is precisely the same as the perception that our mind has of the object, and thus is not a prerequisite of the acquaintance it has of it.

> The second erroneous meaning is that they have simple-mindedly taken the *presence* to be *spatial presence*, such as pertains to bodies. This seems apparent enough in the case of the author of the *Treatise concerning the Search after Truth* himself, since he makes the difficulty that the soul would have in seeing the sun itself to consist in the sun's being so far away, and in its being improbable that the soul should leave its body to go and find the sun in the sky. He therefore regards *spatial distance* as an obstacle which puts a body in the position of not being visible to our mind; therefore, also, it is *spatial presence* which he believes to be necessary for our mind to see its objects.

> However, since false opinions cannot be held together and always contradict themselves somewhere, they say other things which show that this *spatial presence* has nothing to do with it. According to them, supposing God to have allowed our soul to leave our body to go and find the sun in order to see it, its journey would be a complete waste of time. It would not see it any better when it was not only very close, but even inside this star, than it would by staying put. For could our soul be more present to the sun than it is to its own body? Now, according to the author of the *Treatise concerning the Search after Truth* the soul no more sees its own body itself than it sees all the others.

110

Therefore it is in vain that he puts forward as a reason that prevents our soul from seeing the sun itself, that it is at a distance from it and cannot leave its body to go and walk in the sky; since, present or distant, it is the same thing for the soul. So the soul is sentenced irrevocably, by this philosophy of false ideas, never to see any body itself, present or distant, near or far.

(trans. Joanna Wilkinson)

Arnauld's distinction between spatial and objective presence is crucial for an understanding of what has gone wrong in Malebranche's thinking about perception of outer objects. It is because Malebranche has failed to distinguish between objective and spatial presence that he has made 'ideas' into things that come between the perceiver and the perceived. Once the distinction is made it is possible to say, with Arnauld, that the objective presence of an object to our mind 'is precisely the same as the perception that our mind has of the object'. To say that one has an idea of an object is simply a circumlocutary way of saying that one is perceiving (or conceiving) the object. Ideas are not entities that *represent* objects. The representative theory of perception goes out of the window.

Locke has traditionally been thought of as holding the representative theory. Reid says that 'according to the philosophical meaning of the word idea, it does not signify that act of the mind which we call thought or conception, but some object of thought'. He goes on to illustrate this by reference to Locke: 'Ideas, according to Mr. Locke (whose very frequent use of the word has probably been the occasion of its being adopted into common language), "are nothing but the immediate objects of the mind in thinking"'.[2]

This interpretation of Locke, as holding the representative theory, has been increasingly questioned in the last twenty years or so. John Yolton, in the introduction to his abridged edition of Locke's *Essay*, even goes so far as to refer to 'Locke's attempt to use ideas in his theory of knowledge *without* making them into entities' (my emphasis).[3] My own opinion is that Locke, in the *Essay*, simply did not face up to the question whether ideas are acts or entities. He did not make them into either, to the exclusion of the other. In his *Examination of Malebranche's Opinion of Seeing All Things in God* he distinguished between 'acts of perception' and 'ideas perceived'[4], but this was in the course of examining what Malebranche meant by 'sentiment'. It was not a case of Locke, having carefully considered whether ideas are acts or entities, coming down on the side of their being entities. His understanding of the word 'idea' was such that at some time he would write of ideas as acts, at other times as entities. It is *we* who ask whether ideas are acts or entities. From our point of

111

view Locke's use of the term is regrettably imprecise. That is what explains the disagreement as to whether or not he held the representative theory.

It is tempting to suppose that Berkeley got his notion of an idea from Locke. The first sentence of Section 1 of Part 1 of the *Principles of Human Knowledge* is as follows: 'It is evident to anyone who takes a survey of the objects of human knowledge, that they are either ideas actually imprinted on the senses, or else such as are perceived by attending to the passions and operations of the mind, or lastly ideas formed by help of memory and imagination, either compounding, dividing, or barely representing those originally perceived in the aforesaid ways'. This is very reminiscent of the part of Locke's *Essay* in which he distinguished between ideas of sense and ideas of reflection (Bk. II, Ch. 1), and the part in which he says that we get complex ideas by repeating, comparing and uniting simple ideas (Bk. II, Ch. 2). But although Berkeley, in this first section, writes as if he means by 'idea' what Locke meant, it soon emerges that he is operating with a more precise notion. In Section 25 he says that 'all our ideas, sensations, or the things which we perceive... are visibly inactive'. Ideas are inactive precisely because they are not acts of perceiving, thinking, and so on, but *the things which we perceive*. The question that remained open for Locke is not left open by Berkeley. He comes down on the side of ideas being entities.

The question I want to consider is whether Berkeley got his more precise notion of an idea from Malebranche.

Berkeley has an argument in his first major work, *An Essay towards a New Theory of Vision*, that goes something like this:

> Distance being a line directed end-wise to the eye, it projects only one point in the fund of the eye, which point remains invariably the same, whether the distance be longer or shorter (Section 2). So there is nothing in the stimulation of the eyes that varies systematically with the distance of the object, and that could be the physical basis for an immediate visual awareness of distance. Therefore the impression we are under, that we literally *see* things as being near or far off, must be illusory. There must be some ancillary sensation, such as the sensation we get when we squint to see a close object, which we have learnt, from experience, means that the object is close enough to touch (Section 16). Now, someone born blind, but later given sight, would not have the necessary experience of the conjunction of the sensation of squinting with the object being close enough to touch. So the sensation, even if it occurred, would not mean anything to him. It would not suggest closeness, as it does to us. So the object would not

112

seem close, to him. Or at any distance, for that matter. So it would seem to him to be in his mind (Section 41).

I am not concerned with the falsity of the premise that 'there is nothing in the stimulation of the eyes that varies systematically with the distance of the object'. Berkeley can be excused. What scientists call 'stereoacuity' in vision was not discovered until the nineteenth century, by Sir Charles Wheatstone. (In 1838 Wheatstone invented the stereoscope, in which two pictures of an object photographed at slightly different angles are viewed, one by each eye, to yield an image that appears to be three-dimensional.)

What concerns me is the last part of the argument. In Section 46 Berkeley expresses his conclusion in terms of 'outness'. He says:

> From what we have shown it is a manifest consequence that the ideas of space, outness, and things placed at a distance are not, strictly speaking, the object of sight.

Expressed in terms of outness the argument in Section 41 would go like this:

1.   We do *not* immediately see things as being *out from us*.

2.   We do *not* immediately see things as being *out of our minds*.

3.   The things we immediately see are *in our minds*.

That argument, it seems to me, relies on an ambiguity of 'outness', just as Malebranche's argument relies on the ambiguity of 'presence'. The one ambiguity mirrors the other.

It does not follow, of course, that Berkeley's argument was suggested to him by reading Malebranche. It could just be a coincidence. But I do not think it is. There are too many other references to Malebranche in Berkeley's works, including the *Philosophical Commentaries*. Moreover there is that unusual word 'outness'. The definition of it in the *Oxford English Dictionary* captures its ambiguity perfectly. Outness is 'the quality, fact, or condition of being out or external, especially of being external *to the percipient or to the mind*' (my emphasis). Following the definition there are references to Berkeley's *New Theory of Vision*, Section 46, and to his *Principles*, Section 43. Perhaps the authors of the Dictionary thought Berkeley had introduced the word into the English language. If so, they would be wrong. It was a translator of Malebranche's *Search after Truth* who did that, in the sixth of the 'Elucidations[5]. I just cannot believe that Berkeley, independently, thought up such an unusual word. He got it from Malebranche, via Taylor's 1694 translation of the *Search*. A copy of the second edition of this translation, with '1701' inscribed in ink on the cover, was in the library of Trinity College, Dublin, where Berkeley graduated in 1704. The ambiguity of Malebranche's 'presence' is the pattern for the ambiguity of Berkeley's 'outness'. In short, Berkeley got his notion of an idea, not from Locke, but from Malebranche.

Why, then, did Berkeley write as he did in the first section of the *Principles*? I can only suppose that he wanted to be thought of in connection with Locke, rather than in connection with Malebranche. He may have thought that his philosophy would be more likely to get attention if it were presented as a *reductio ad absurdum* of Locke's principles than if it were presented in the context of Malebranche's. There were things in Malebranche's philosophy - principally the doctrine of 'seeing all things in God', but also the occasionalist analysis of voluntary movement - that were unacceptable this side of the English Channel. Hume was later to say, of Malebranche's theory of 'the universal energy and operation of the Supreme Being': 'We are got into fairy land, long ere we have reached the last steps of our theory'.[6] In the footnote he remarked that the theory had no authority in England. It would be perfectly understandable if Berkeley were to play down the Malebranchian ancestry of his notion of 'idea', and present his philosophy, instead, as if he was starting from Lockean principles. Locke, at the time, was the person to whom to relate, not Malebranche.

Are there other aspects of Berkeley's philosophy that have a Malebranchian ancestry? I believe there are.

Malebranche asked himself the question: what is the cause of our ideas? He considered five possible answers, three of which are: (i) our ideas are directly caused by external objects; (ii) they are directly caused by God; also, God creates external objected in accordance with His ideas of them; (iii) there is only one set of ideas of external objects, God's, but we exist in God and 'see all things in him', i.e. we have a share in His ideas; also, God creates external objects in accordance with His ideas of them. Malebranche preferred (iii) to (i) on religious grounds, and (iii) to (ii) on grounds of economy (there is only one set of ideas needed).

It may be objected: if economy is a good reason for preferring (iii) to (ii) why should it not be a good reason for omitting the final bits of (ii) and (iii) ('also, God creates external objects in accordance with His ideas of them')?

Malebranche's answer to this objection was that, while we cannot be absolutely sure that God did create external objects, (a) we have nothing that proves to us that there are *not* any such objects, and (b) we have a strong inclination to believe there *are*.

I believe that some of the key features of Berkeley's immaterialist philosophy can be presented as a reaction to Malebranche's thinking.

114

First, Berkeley rejected Malebranche's 'seeing all things in God' doctrine as incomprehensible (*Principles*, Section 148). Secondly, he held that economy *is* a good reason for not postulating external objects. 'God might have done everything as well without them' (*Principles*, Section 53). Thirdly, he held that we *do* have something that proves to us that there are not any external objects; namely, that the concept of material substance involves a contradiction (*Principles*, Section 7). Fourthly, he held that it can be questioned whether ordinary people have a strong inclination to believe in the existence of material objects (*Philosophical Commentaries* 686). If they do have such an inclination, Berkeley thinks, it is because they illegitimately abstract the *existence* of sensible things from their being *perceived* (*Principles*, Sections 4-5).

Berkeley's immaterialism is Malebranche's philosophy minus the external world and minus our 'seeing all things in God'. Malebranche, he held, was right about the objects of perception being ideas. But he was wrong both about our seeing God's ideas, and about God having created things to correspond to His ideas. God causes us to have out ideas of things, according to the ideas He has, but without actually having created any material things to correspond to them (*Principles*, Sections 25-35).

Notes

1. *Father Malebranche's Treatise concerning The Search after Truth*, trans. T. Taylor, Oxford, 1694, p. 114.

2. Thomas Reid, *Essays on the Intellectual Powers of Man*, edited and abridged by A. D. Woozley, London: Macmillan, 1941, p. 12.

3. John Locke, *An Essay Concerning Human Understanding*, abridged and edited with an introduction by John W. Yolton, London: Dent, 1977, p. xxi.

4. *The Works of John Locke*, with a preliminary essay and notes by J. A. St. John, London: Bell, 1889, Vol. II, p. 437.

5. *Father Malebranche's Treatise concerning the Search after Truth*, p. 122.

6. Hume, *An Enquiry concerning Human Understanding*, 1748, Sect. VII, Pt. I, para. 57.

9   Hume's Criticism of Malebranche's Theory of Causation: A Lesson in the Historiography of Philosophy

JOHN P. WRIGHT

The importance of Hume's reading of the philosophy of Malebranche in the formation of his own thought has been stressed by a number of twentieth-century scholars. Indeed, the letter which was discovered in the early 1960's from Hume to his youthful friend Michael Ramsay[1] only served to confirm what a variety of scholars had written earlier about the close connection of certain ideas of these two philosophers. In this letter Hume mentioned Malebranche's *Recherche de la Vérité* first among four books which he recommended for an understanding of the 'metaphysical Parts' of his reasoning in his *Treatise of Human Nature.* But in an article published in 1916 in the *Philosophical Review* C.W. Doxee had already stressed what he called the 'identical doctrines' taught by these two thinkers[2] These included '(a) a very similar analysis of causation; (b) a negative account of the knowability of the self; and (c) a doctrine of "natural judgment"'. Doxee sought to show that the relation between the two thinkers gave a good 'illustration of the way important ideas arise and develop.' Writing in 1938 in the *Revue Internationale de Philosophie*, R.W. Church set out to show that Malebranche 'anticipated and contributed' to doctrines which are 'too widely thought of as having originated wholly with Hume'[3] He discussed 'the probable influence' of Malebranche's discussion of the soul on Hume's account of personal identity, as well as the influence of the account of causality. In their well-known books on Hume writers such as John Laird[4] and Charles Hendel[5] as well as Church himself[6] sought to show the influence of Malebranche on central Humean doctrines. In his fine recent study of

Malebranche and British Philosophy Charles McCracken has continued this tradition by arguing that the French philosopher was a 'seminal source of British ideas in the eighteenth century' - particularly those of Hume, Berkeley and Reid.[7] McCracken has added to earlier lists of ideas which the two philosophers shared in showing that 'Hume could find in this alien thinker much that he took to be true' (p. 289).

While all the scholars I have mentioned stressed the influence or possible influence of the doctrines of Malebranche on those of Hume they also noted some differences - especially in their theories of causation. Indeed, they have based their remarks on Hume's own explicit criticisms of Malebranche's occasionalist theory of causation in the *Treatise of Human Nature*[8] and in his *Enquiry Concerning Human Understanding*[9]. In the latter work Hume made fun of philosophers who think that 'every thing is full of God'. He wrote that 'we are got into fairy land, long ere' we reach the last stages of the theory (pp. 71-72). In general, twentieth-century scholars have maintained that while Hume accepted Malebranche's view that there is no necessary connection between natural causes and their effects, he rejected categorically the latter's claim that the Deity is the sole cause in the universe.[10] McCracken wrote that Malebranche and Hume only differed in their answer to the question whether there is more to our notion of causal 'necessity' or power than a belief based on a habitual association of sensations. He argued that

> For Hume, the sum and substance of causal necessity is just our irresistible *feeling* that the one event must follow the other. To Malebranche, on the other hand, there is an objective causal necessity; the necessity that any event willed by God accompany his willing it.
>
> (McCracken, p. 265)

In articulating the difference between the two thinkers in this way McCracken has accepted the view generally held by philosophers that for Hume there is no objective causal necessity and that the only necessity which exists in the universe belongs to the mind of the observer of constant succession.

In this paper I shall argue that a more careful attention to Hume's criticism of Malebranche will yield a very different view of his own theory of causation, and more generally of his ontology and epistemology. I argue in particular that far from agreeing with Malebranche that there is no natural objective necessary connection, Hume set out to develop a philosophical response to his causal theory which allowed for the existence of such a connection. I believe that the historians of philosophy to which I have referred have concentrated too much on the task of showing the *influence* of the ideas of the earlier thinker on the later one, and not sufficiently taken into account the lessons which can be learned from a precise description of Hume's *critical* assessment of Malebranche's view. At the same time, I do not want to deny the similarity of doctrines of the two thinkers. Indeed, I think that by examining Hume's development of a doctrine suggested in Malebranche's *Recherche* – the doctrine of 'natural judgment' - we can reach a deeper understanding of what is generally understood as the positive side of his project in the first Book of the *Treatise of Human Nature*. Hume showed that when we apply this doctrine to our natural judgments of causation then we have a sceptical justification of our natural inclination to believe in real necessary connections between the finite objects which we find constantly conjoined. Thus, even Hume's positive development of this Malebranchist theory is used to undermine what, in his *Enquiry Concerning Human Understanding*, he called 'the foundation' of all Malebranche's philosophy (p. 73).

I. Provinces of Divine Intellect and Will in Malebranche and Hume

There are two central Malebranchist doctrines which Hume explicitly sought to refute in his philosophical writings - his doctrine of moral relations and his doctrine of occasional causes. In his *Enquiry Concerning the Principles of Morals* Hume expressed the view that Malebranche originated 'the abstract theory of morals' which 'excludes all sentiment, and pretends to found everything on reason.' According to this theory all right is 'founded on certain *rapports* or relations.'[11] In fact, Malebranche held that moral truths are based on the intrinsic nature of things, no less than the truths of mathematics. In his *Traité de Morale* Malebranche wrote that

> God sees as well as I that 2 times 2 makes 4 and that triangles which are on the same base, and which are between the same parallels are equal. I can also discover, at least confusedly, the *relations of perfection*, which are between these same ideas; and these relations make an immutable *order* which God consults when he acts: this is an order which ought also to regulate the esteem and love of all intelligences.[12]

On his view the will of God is subservient to these objective moral relations. It is no more possible to deny that two times two make four than to deny that a 'beast is more estimable than a stone, and less estimable than a man.' In both cases the opposite is inconceivable. For Malebranche, morality is based on 'relations of perfection' which arise from a comparison of their intrinsic natures (p. 21, Sects. XII and XIII).

Malebranche's account of the ontological status of truths about causal connection is very different. These are not bound up with truths

118

about the intrinsic natures of what is supposed to be connected. In his dispute with Foucher, Malebranche wrote that

> There are two kinds of unchangeable truths. There are those which are unchangeable by their nature or by themselves such as two plus two make four; and there are others which are unchangeable because they have been determined by the will of God, who is not subject to change - such as that one ball moves another in encountering it.[13]

While Malebranche argued for his theory that there are no real causes in nature on epistemological grounds, such a passage suggests that, at bottom, the reason we find no necessary connections between cause and effect is that unlike the truths of mathematics and morality these depend upon the free legislation of the creator. It is true that God always acts in the simplest ways, by general laws, and in terms of what Leibniz called the principle of sufficient reason. But, as McCracken states, like Leibniz, Malebranche held that God 'could have decreed other laws to govern the nature of things.'[14]

Hume set out to refute the Malebranchist doctrine of moral relations at the beginning of Book 3 of his *Treatise of Human Nature* and in the first Appendix to his *Enquiry Concerning the Principles of Morals*. At the end of the Appendix Hume gave what I take to be one of the clearest expressions of his own ontological views. These views are expressed in theological language and can be directly compared with those of Malebranche. In this passage Hume distinguished the respective provinces of taste - (which for him included moral good and evil) and reason. He wrote that the standard of reason

> being founded on the nature of things, is eternal and inflexible, even by the will of the Supreme Being: the standard of [taste], arising from the internal frame and constitution of animals, is ultimately derived from that Supreme Will, which bestowed on each being its peculiar nature, and arranged the several classes and orders of existence. (p. 294)

Hume's ontological distinction between the objects of reason and taste presupposes a distinction between God's intellect and will which we have just found in Malebranche's writings. Unlike Malebranche, Hume holds that the Divine Will just happens to have created a set of beings who react with moral approval to some situations and with moral disapproval to others. There is nothing in the intrinsic nature of things makes us regard with moral indifference the fact that 'a young tree, over-tops and destroys its parent' while we see the most heinous crime in Nero's murder of his mother (p. 293). Hume says there is the same objective relation in both cases.

While Hume clearly opposed Malebranche's view that moral distinctions are rooted in the intrinsic nature of things his view of mathematical truths is similar to that of the French philosopher. In his *Enquiry Concerning Hume Understanding* Hume wrote that '*three times five is equal to the half of thirty,* expresses a relation between these numbers', that such propositions are discoverable merely by reason and that they are 'without dependence on what is anywhere existent in the universe' (p. 25). But what are we to say about causal relations? On Hume's view these relations are the basis for all our reasonings about matters of fact. Given Hume's distinction between reason and taste does this not mean that they are 'founded on the nature of things' and are 'eternal and inflexible by the Will of the Supreme Being'?

I believe that Hume's views on the ontological status of causal necessity are as different from those of Malebranche as are his views on the ontological status of morality. There are good grounds to think that while Malebranche ascribed causality to the Divine Will or order of existence, Hume thought the relation had its foundation in God's intellect or, in other words, in the nature of things. The passage I have been examining from his moral *Enquiry* provides further circumstantial evidence in support of my reading. For, just prior to the part I have quoted, Hume wrote that reason leads us through 'circumstances and relations, known or *supposed*... to the discovery of the concealed and unknown' (p. 294, my italics). There are good grounds to think that the relation which is supposed here is one of causal necessity. The notion that we 'suppose' certain things played an important role in Hume's epistemology; while he denied that we have any idea of objective causal necessity, he stated that we 'suppose' such a necessity between cause and effect when we experience objects as constantly conjoined.[15] In his account of scientific reasoning in his *Enquiry Concerning Human Understanding*, Hume asserted that scientists operate on the basis of a maxim that 'the connexion between all causes and effects is equally necessary' and that it is this supposition which leads them - in spite of apparent irregularities in experience - to the discovery of unknown causes (p. 87; cf. *Treatise*, p. 132). Put together, these passages suggest that, in his account of reason in the Appendix to his *Enquiry Concerning the Principles of Morals*, Hume intended to include causal reasoning. And if this is right, then, when we employ such reasoning, we suppose a relation in the nature of things which precedes the Divine will or actual order of existence.

II. Hume's Criticism of Malebranche's Causal Theory

Let me now turn to Hume's own explicit discussion of the occasionalist theory of causation in his *Treatise* and explain why I believe it shows that there are objective necessary connections. This discussion occurs in the section of the *Treatise* entitled 'Of the idea of necessary connection'; in this section Hume returned to the main question posed in Part 3 of Book 1, namely the question '*What is our idea of necessity, when we say that two objects are necessarily connected together*' (p. 155; cf. pp. 77-78). From the beginning of the section it is clear that he identifies the idea of necessary connection with that of power or force - an identification which was explicitly made by Malebranche and by few other writers of the period.[16] It is in this section where Hume identifies the origin of this idea as an internal impression which arises from custom and habit, and explains how we project this impression on to objects.

The central difficulty which confronts anyone who attempts to discover Hume's own ontology of causation is that his discussions of this relation are primarily epistemological. However, the importance of Hume's discussion of Malebranche's theory lies in the fact Malebranche had himself drawn an ontological conclusion from an account of the *idea* of causality which they both shared. In rejecting the conclusion about natural causation which Malebranche drew, Hume revealed his own ontological views about causation.

Hume began his criticism of Malebranche's occasionalism by pointing out that modern philosophers are agreed that we never discover the power which is involved in causation and that 'tis in vain we search for it in all the known qualities of matter.' He notes that 'the Cartesians' (a footnote to the *Recherche* on the previous page suggests that it was primarily Malebranche's discussion which Hume had in mind) conclude from the further premise that 'we are perfectly acquainted with the essence of matter' that it itself is 'endow'd with no efficacy, and that 'tis impossible for it of itself to communicate motion, or produce any of those effects, which we ascribe to it' (*Treatise*, p. 159). This argument may be represented as follows:

1.   We have no idea of power or necessary connection in matter.

2.   We are perfectly acquainted with the essence of matter; in other words, our idea of matter gives us an accurate account of the nature of things.

3.   Hence, matter itself is entirely devoid of power or necessary connection.

In this Malebranchist argument an ontological conclusion about the nature of things is drawn from a premise about ideas. Now it is important to recognize that while Hume accepts the first premise he rejects the conclusion. To see this we need to understand Hume's criticism of the complete occasionalist view.

Hume notes that, having concluded on the basis of our ideas that matter is entirely inert, the Cartesians went on to argue that since the power which produces the effects which are evident to our senses must exist somewhere, 'it must lie in the DEITY, or that divine being, who contains in his nature all excellency and perfection' (*Treatise*, p. 159). Malebranche had argued that the Divine Will, being omnipotent, is necessarily connected with each of its effects, and that hence all power is placed in the Deity. This claim was for him closely bound up with divine attributes such as simplicity and universality. Indeed, Malebranche expresses his view as the view that laws themselves 'are efficacious', that 'they act, whereas bodies cannot act' (*Search*, p. 449). But, in *his* account Hume wrote that he would disregard the details of the theory since the central question is whether we have any clearer idea of power in the Deity than in body. He argues that we do not. Since every idea is derived from a corresponding impression, and we have no innate idea of the Deity, it follows that any idea of Divine power must be derived from 'some instances... wherein this power *is perceiv'd* to exert itself' (*Treatise*, p. 160). Since we find 'no impression, either of sensation or reflection, (which) implies any force or efficacy' it is impossible to form any general idea of activity or force in the Divine being.

It is at this point where Hume's argument becomes central for our purposes. For he then notes that the Cartesians should have drawn a parallel argument to that which they drew in the case of matter:

> Since these philosophers... have concluded, that matter cannot be endow'd with any efficacious principle, because 'tis impossible to discover in it such a principle; the same course of reasoning shou'd determine them to exclude it from the supreme being. (*Treatise*, p. 160)

Thus we can construct the argument the Cartesians are led to in the following way:

1. We have no idea of power or necessary connection through our idea of matter or of the supreme being.

2. We are acquainted with the essence of matter and with the essence of the supreme being through our ideas.

3. Hence, there is no power or necessity either in matter or in the supreme being.

This conclusion, it should be noted, is fundamentally the conclusion which was ascribed to Hume by Charles McCracken in the passage we examined earlier - the conclusion that there is no objective power in the universe. But, in fact, Hume wrote that this conclusion really is 'absurd and impious'. He considered this argument as a *reductio ad absurdum* of the Cartesian view that we can conclude that there is no activity in reality because we discover none in our ideas. But he says that the occasionalists can avoid the absurd conclusion by recognizing 'from the very first, that they have no adequate idea of power or efficacy in any object', that is, 'neither in body or spirit.' This view seems to be that of Hume himself. It involves the rejection of the second premise of the above argument. Hume rejects the Cartesian view that we can determine the nature of reality through our idea of matter.

In Part IV of his *Treatise* Hume returned to a discussion of the Malebranchist theory of causation when he considered the question whether we can say that motions in the body are 'the cause of thought and perception'. He presented a 'dilemma' which once again makes it clear that he considered real objective power as an alternative to occasionalism. The dilemma is

> either to assert, that nothing can be the cause of another, but where the mind can perceive the connexion in its idea of the objects: Or to maintain, that all objects, which we find constantly conjoin'd, are upon that account to be regarded as causes and effects.

Hume again points out that in embracing the former alternative the occasionalists 'in reality affirm, that there is no such thing in the universe as a cause or productive principle...' We have already seen that earlier in the *Treatise* he entirely rejects this conclusion. Thus, he writes that

> we are necessarily reduc'd to the other side of the dilemma, *viz.* that all objects, which are found to be constantly conjoin'd, are upon that account only to be regarded as causes and effects.

But what does this mean? Given the alternatives of the dilemma it clearly means that we ascribe 'a productive principle' to the objects merely on the basis of an experienced conjunction. In the particular case at issue in this section it means that we affirm on the basis of an experienced succession of motions and dispositions of the body followed by corresponding states of mind that the former really do produce the latter. And this, wrote Hume, 'evidently gives the advantage to the materialists above their antagonists' (*Treatise*, pp. 248-50). It does so because it implies that there really is a genuine necessary connection between the state of the body and the corresponding mental state.

A footnote to his discussion of occasionalism in his later *Enquiry Concerning Human Understanding* provides further evidence that Hume intended his refutation of the Malebranchist position as a way of allowing for the existence of real but unknown powers in matter. Here Hume referred to 'MALEBRANCHE and other CARTESIANS' who made the 'doctrine of the universal and sole efficacy of the Deity' the 'foundation of all their philosophy'. However, the overall discussion, which appeared in an earlier version in his *A Letter from a Gentleman to his friend in Edinburgh*, suggests that Hume was thinking far more about British than French philosophy when he wrote it. In his *Letter* Hume insisted that, in spite of the views of some of his followers, Newton himself rejected the occasionalist theory 'by substituting the Hypothesis of an Aetherial Fluid, not the immediate volition of the Deity, as the cause of Attraction'.[17] This theme is taken up at the beginning of the footnote of the *Enquiry* where (in the original version) Hume commended Newton for putting forward the hypothesis of an 'etherial active matter to explain his universal Attraction'.[18] Hume noted that British philosophers such as Locke, Clarke and Cudworth don't even consider the occasionalist theory and 'suppose all along that matter has a real, though subordinate and derived power'. He ended by asking why the occasionalist doctrine has become so popular 'among our modern metaphysicians' (*Enquiry*, p. 73). In using this expression, Hume may well have had in mind George Berkeley, whose *Siris* appeared in 1744 at the time Hume was in England writing his book on *Human Understanding*. Berkeley wrote in *Siris* that all talk of 'forces residing in bodies... is to be regarded only as a mathematical hypothesis, and not as anything really existing in nature'.[19] He clearly expressed the Malebranchist doctrine of causation when he wrote that the task of natural scientist is 'only to discover the laws of nature, that is, the general rules and methods of motion, and to account for particular phenomena by reducing them under, or shewing their conformity to, such general rules' (#231). Unlike Hume, Berkeley interpreted the Newtonian ether as a mere 'instrument or medium' by which 'the real Agent' - the Deity - acts on 'grosser bodies' (#221).

It is important to realize that none of the passages I have looked at in any way mitigates Hume's own firm conclusion that we have absolutely *no idea* of power or necessary connection. At the same time, it would be wrong to think that Hume fails to provide any criterion for what would constitute an objective causal connection. While he followed Malebranche in considering necessary connection as identical to causal power, in his rejection of the Malebranchist theory of Divine causation he developed a very different interpretation of what constituted real causal necessity. For Malebranche, the only necessary connection in the universe is that between the decrees of an infinite will and the effects which are brought about in nature: it is impossible that an infinite will can act, and that which it wills not to occur. But, as we have seen, Hume denied that this abstract relation gives us any insight into causal power. We must, he wrote, conceive of this power as existing 'in some particular being'. Hume claimed that the 'true manner of conceiving a particular power in a particular body' is to 'conceive the connexion between the cause and effect' in such a way that we should 'be able to pronounce, from a simple view of the one, that it must be follow'd or preceded by the other' (*Treatise*, p. 161). Earlier in his discussion Hume noted that if we had genuine knowledge of causation we would be able to penetrate into 'the essences' of those objects we call cause and effect and determine that the one is dependent on the other. This 'wou'd imply the absolute contradiction and impossibility of conceiving any thing different' (p. 87). Of course, Hume denied that we ever have such knowledge of causation. Nevertheless, it is clear that he conceived of such knowledge as being like that which we have in mathematics - as being founded on the absolute nature of things. Unlike Malebranche, Hume held that genuine causal connection involves a real intelligible connection between the relata. This confirms what was said earlier about the different provinces of causality in the Divine nature for the two philosophers.

III. Hume's Adaptation of Malebranche's Suggestions Concerning an Epistemology of Natural Judgement

Hume clearly thought that, even though we have no genuine idea of objective necessity, we naturally suppose that there are necessary connections in the world. In his *Enquiry Concerning Human Understanding* he wrote that after we experience two objects constantly conjoined,

> We then call the one object, *Cause*; the other, *Effect*. We suppose that there is some connexion between them; some power in the one, by which it infallibly produces the other, and operates with the greatest certainty and strongest necessity. (*Enquiries*, p. 75)

Thus, we need to ask just what we are doing when we ascribe a productive principle on the basis of constant conjunction and why we should consider this inference or judgment to have any validity. I believe that we can reach a deeper understanding of Hume's account when we see just how he has developed a theory of natural judgment which he probably found in the writings of Malebranche.

First, let me briefly summarize Hume's own account of causal judgment. While he holds that our idea of necessary connection has its origin in a mere impression which is produced in the mind through a constant succession, he also believes that we normally disregard this fact. In the chapter on necessary connection in his *Treatise* he sought to explain how the impression of necessity is projected on to external objects. He explains how, through an association of ideas, the mind develops 'a great propensity to spread itself on external objects, and to conjoin with them any internal impressions, which they occasion' (p. 167). Later on he accounts for the belief in objective necessity simply through custom itself: 'because custom has render'd it difficult to separate the ideas, [we] are apt to fancy such a separation to be in itself

125

impossible and absurd' (p. 223). On this account we simply mistake the subjective association of ideas caused by the constant conjunction for a real intelligible connection between cause and effect. Because we can't think of the idea of the effect apart from that of the cause we think we actually perceive an objective necessary connection between them. This account is repeated in the *Enquiry Concerning Human Understanding* (pp. 75-76). But in either case the question arises how we can conceive such judgments to give us *any* valid conception of reality. For when we examine the judgment itself in a philosophical or reflective state of mind, we see that we are naturally led to disregard the contents of the actual ideas which are involved in its formation. As Hume keeps stressing, our idea of necessity has its origin in an internal impression of the mind which results from the experience of a constant succession. How can we give any epistemic value to such judgments which either mistakenly project an internal impression on to external objects or mistake a subjective association for a real intelligible connection in the objects?

To answer this question it is useful to examine Malebranche's theory of natural judgment. This theory is elaborate and I can only touch on it here. Malebranche used it to explain how we form quite correct judgments about the objects of our senses - for example, the judgment that an object moving away from us remains the same size in spite of the fact that the image of it in our visual field grows smaller. The judgment is based partly on another sensation, for example, that which we have of the angles formed by our two eyes as the point of focus moves away from us. Malebranche says that such a judgment is formed through a 'compound sensation' (*Search*, p. 34). But he thought that we also form natural judgments which are in themselves partly false, such as the judgment that the objects we immediately perceive are independent of us. He wrote that 'we have no sensation of external objects that does not include some false judgment' (*Search*, pp. 67-68). While it is not false that there are external objects corresponding to our sensations, it is quite false that our sensations of colour or sound are actually in the objects, or that the pain we feel is actually in the hand. Yet such judgments, like that of size constancy are made 'within us, ...independently of us, and even in spite of us'. They are distinguished from the free judgments of the will which form the basis of science and philosophy.

There is an important development of this theory in the Sixth Eclaircissement of the *Recherche* where Malebranche discussed Descartes' proof for the existence of bodies. In Books 1 and 2 Malebranche asserted that we form a natural judgment that what we sense is external to us (*Search*, pp. 58-59, 88). According to Malebranche, while Descartes was wrong in thinking that we can actually demonstrate their existence, we can still show that it is 'entirely probable' on the basis of natural judgment. (*Search*, pp. 573-

74). We have, he argues, a very 'strong propensity to believe that there are bodies surrounding us' and unlike the sensible qualities we experience we cannot show that the bodies themselves cannot exist independently. Malebranche suggests that we are *justified* in believing that which we have a strong inclination to believe in so far as that belief is not opposed to reason:

> We have nothing that proves to us there are not any [external bodies], and on the contrary we have a strong inclination to believe that there are bodies. We have, then, more reason to believe that there are bodies than to believe there are not any. Thus, it seems that *we should believe there are bodies: for we are naturally led to follow our natural judgment when we cannot positively correct it through light or evidence.* (My emphasis.)

Malebranche concluded that we should believe that there are external objects but deny that they contain the sensible qualities which we naturally believe exist in them.

I believe that it was this epistemic theory - undeveloped, and hesitant as it was - which Hume himself developed when he sought to found the sciences on human nature in the first Book of his *Treatise* and in his *Enquiry Concerning Human Understanding*. At the end of the *Treatise* section 'Of scepticism with regard to the senses' Hume wrote that he sought to conclude that 'we ought to have an implicit faith in our senses' but that he found himself unable to draw this conclusion because he could not see 'how such trivial qualities of the fancy, conducted by such false suppositions' can lead to any solid and rational system (*Treatise*, p. 217). He clearly thought he was more successful in his attempt to found the belief in causality in this way. At the beginning of the section 'Of the modern philosophy' he formulated his goal as that of founding the understanding on those 'principles which are permanent, irresistable, and universal; such as the customary transition from causes to effects, and from effects to causes' (p. 225). Even more clearly, in the conclusion to the *Enquiry*, Hume stated that his own academic philosophy was based on the recognition that nothing can free us from scepticism but 'the strong power of natural instinct'. He then appealed to the principle that 'philosophical decisions are nothing but the reflections of common life, methodized and corrected' (p. 162). This, it seems to me, is a clear expression of the principle which we have seen hesitantly suggested in the sixth Eclaircissement of Malebranche's *Recherche*.

Hume held that our causal judgments are based on a strong and universal inclination to believe that items which are constantly conjoined are causally related. But he also held that our most natural belief in necessary connection is faulty. At the end of his discussion in the section of the *Treatise* entitled 'Of the ancient philosophy' Hume wrote that it is 'natural for men in their common and careless way of thinking, to imagine they perceive a connexion betwixt such objects as they have constantly found united together' (*Treatise*, pp. 222-23). But, of course, reason shows us that we perceive no such thing. This error is correctable by philosophers who 'discover that there is no *known* connexion among objects' (my italics). Yet, Hume still says that the 'true philosophy approaches nearer to the sentiments of the vulgar'. I believe that what he means is that the true philosopher allows the *existence* of such a necessary connection even though she recognizes that we never have a perception of it. Taking up Malebranche's hints in the sixth Eclaircissement, Hume thinks that we ought to believe what we are strongly inclined to believe after that belief is corrected by reason.

Conclusion

Thus, in the final analysis, we see that Hume employed a suggestion of Malebranche (the suggestion concerning justification of natural judgment) to undermine what he considered to be the foundation of all Malebranche's philosophy (the theory of occasional causes). The lesson we learn from a careful analysis of both Hume's criticism of Malebranche and his use of Malebranche's ideas is that he himself was devising a philosophical system which allowed for the existence of objective natural necessity and showed how our natural judgment of this necessity could be provided with a sceptical justification. A careful account of his critical reaction to the views of Malebranche establishes that Hume's own philosophical belief concerning the ontological status of causal necessity is directly contrary to that which is generally ascribed to him.[20]

Notes

1. Tadeusz Koznecki, 'Dawida Hume 'a Nieznane Listy W Zbiorach Muzeum Czartoryskick (Polska)', *Archiwum Historii Filozofii I Mysli Spolecznej*, 9 (1963), 127-39; reprinted in Richard Popkin, 'So Hume did read Berkeley', *Journal of Philosophy*, 61 (1964), 773-78. Hume refers to Malebranche's *Recherche de la Vérité*. His own copy of the third edition of this work is housed today in the library of the University of Edinburgh.

2. C.W. Doxee, 'Hume's Relation to Malebranche', *Philosophical Review* 25 (1916), 692-710; see esp. pp. 692-93.

3. R.W. Church, 'Malebranche and Hume', *Revue Internationale de Philosophie*, 1 (1938), 143-61; see esp. p. 143.

4. John Laird, *Hume's Philosophy of Human Nature* (London, 1932).

5.   Charles Hendel, *Studies in the Philosophy of David Hume* (Princeton, 1925).

6.   Ralph W. Church, *Hume's Theory of Knowledge* (Ithaca, 1935).

7.   Charles McCracken, *Malebranche and British Philosophy* (Oxford, 1983, p. 20.

8.   David Hume, *A Treatise of Human Nature*, ed. L.A. Selby-Bigge, 2nd edition, revised by P. H. Nidditch (Oxford, 1978), esp. pp. 158-60 and pp. 248-49.

9.   In *Enquiries Concerning Human Understanding and Concerning the Principles of Morals*, ed. L.A. Selby-Bigge, 3rd edition, revised by P. H. Nidditch (Oxford, 1975), pp. 70-73.

10.   See, for example, D. Radner, *Malebranche, A Study of a Cartesian System* (Assen, 1978), p. 40 and Jean Theau, 'La critique de la causalité chez Malebranche et chez Hume', *Dialogue* 15 (1976), p. 549.

11.   In op. cit. in note 9 above, p. 197n.

12.   Nicolas Malebranche, *Traité de morale*, ed. Michel Adam, 2nd ed. *Oeuvres de Malebranche* (Paris, 1975), p. 19, sect. VI. The translation is my own.

13.   In Nicolas Malebranche, *Recherche de la Verité*, ed. G. Rodis-Lewis, 3 vols. *Oeuvres de Malebranche* (Paris, 1963), Vol. 2, pp. 488-89, my translation. The polemic against Foucher formed a Preface to the second volume of the first three editions of the *Recherche*. As mentioned in Note 1, Hume owned the third edition of the *Recherche*.

14.   McCracken, p. 262. McCracken goes so far as to write that Malebranchist laws of nature hold because of God's 'arbitrary decree'. There certainly seem to be tendencies in Malebranche's thought in this direction. After acknowledging that the laws of motion can only be determined through experience he wrote that they *appear* to depend on 'a purely arbitrary act of the will of God' (*Oeuvres Complètes*, Vol. 17-1, p. 53). Tom Lennon appears to read this as an ontological claim when he states that according to Malebranche 'physical laws are arbitrary' (see his 'Philosophical Commentary' appended to the translation of the *Search After Truth*, p. 809). I believe that Lennon wrongly interprets this as leading to a view later adopted by Hume.

15.   *Enquiries*, p. 75; my italics. See my 'Hume's Academic Scepticism: A Reappraisal of his Philosophy of Human Understanding', *Canadian Journal of Philosophy*, 16 (1986), pp. 407-36, esp. Sects. III and IV.

16. *Treatise*, p. 157; cf. Nicolas Malebranche, *The Search After Truth*, trans. T.M. Lennon and P.J. Olscamp (Columbus, 1980), p. 450. See also my *Sceptical Realism of David Hume* (Manchester, 1983), p. 139 and 180 fn. 25.

17. David Hume, *A Letter from a Gentleman to his Friend in Edinburgh* (Edinburgh, 1745); reprinted with an introduction by Ernest Mossner and John V. Price (Edinburgh, 1967), pp. 28-29).

18. David Hume, *Philosophical Essays Concerning Human Understanding*, 2nd. edition (London: A. Millar, 1750), p. 119. I have discussed the change in Hume's text and the reasons for it in my *Sceptical Realism of David Hume*, pp. 162-63.

19. George Berkeley, *Siris...* (Dublin, 1744); reprinted in George Berkeley, *The Works*, ed. A.A. Luce and T.E. Jessop, 9 volumes (Edinburgh, 1948-57).

20. The basic thesis adopted in this paper was first developed by me in the book to which I have referred in notes 16 and 18. For a recent support of the 'realist' interpretation of Hume on causality see Galen Strawson, *The Secret Connexion* (Oxford, 1989).

Malebranche: His Critics and Successors. A Bibliography

Compiled by Stuart Brown

Preliminary Note

This bibliography is not intended to cover the whole Malebranche literature but only what is relevant to the theme of this volume. In compiling it I have used a range of primary and secondary sources, including the bibliographies of Robinet and Sebba listed below. In the list of primary texts I have included Malebranche's main works but I have not sought to list all the editions and éclaircissements, for which the reader may turn to the *Oeuvres Complètes*. I have, however, sought to include a fairly comprehensive list of works relating to Malebranche in the author's own lifetime. I have been sparing in my choice of Leibniz writings relating to Malebranche, since the reader interested in these may be referred to Robinet's *Leibniz et Malebranche*.

The bibliography tries to represent the eighteenth century literature on Malebranche, at least in France, Italy and the English-speaking world. But I have not sought to represent the reception of Malebranche in the nineteenth century since that period (unlike the eighteenth century) is systematically covered by the final volume of the *Oeuvres Complètes*.

I	PRIMARY TEXTS

(A)	WORKS ORIGINATING DURING MALEBRANCHE'S WRITING CAREER (1674-1715)
1674	**Malebranche** (Nicolas), *De la Recherche de la verité où l'on traitte de la nature de l'esprit de l'homme, et de l'usage qu'ol en doit faire pour éviter l'erreur des sciences*, Vol. I (Paris: Pralard). [OCM I]
1675	**Foucher** (Simon), *Critique de la Recherche de la verité où l'on examine en même-tems une partie des Principes de Mr Descartes . Lettre, par un Academicien* (Paris: Martin Courstelier). [Reprinted 1969 with a new introduction by Richard A. Watson (New York: Johnson Reprint, 1969)]

1675   **Desgabets** (Robert), *Critique de la "Critique de la Recherche de la vérité," où l'on découvre le chemin que conduit aux connoissances solids. Pour servir de réponse à la Lettre d'un académicien* (Paris: Du Puis).

1675   **Malebranche** (Nicolas), *De la Recherche de la verité etc.*, Vol. II (Paris: Pralard). [OCM II]

1675   **Malebranche** (Nicolas), *Conversations chrétiennes* (Paris: Gaspard Migeot). [OCM IV]

1676   **Foucher** (Simon), *Réponse pour la Critique à la Préface du second volume de la Recherche de la vérité, où, l'on examine le sentiment de M. Descartes touchant les idées, avec plusieurs remarques utiles pour les sciences* (Paris: Angot).

1677   **Malebranche** (Nicolas), *Méditations pour se disposer à l'humilité et à la pénitence avec quelques considerations de pieté pour tous les jours de la semaine* (Paris: Roulland).

1679   **Foucher** (Simon), *Nouvelle Dissertation sur la Recherche de la Vérité...Contenant la réponse à la "Critique de la Critique de la Recherche de la Vérité"*, etc. (Paris: de la Caille).

1680   **De la Ville** (Louis), *Sentiments de M. Descartes touchant l'essence et la proprieté des corps opposés à ceux de l'Église.* (Paris: Michallet).

1680   **Malebranche** (Nicolas), *Traité de la Nature et de la Grâce* (Amsterdam: Daniel Elsevier).

1681   (8 July) **Bossuet** (Jacques-Begnine), Lettre a Monsieur l'abbé Nicaise. *Correspondance*, ed. Urbain et Levesque 2: 242-244.

[1681]   **Fénelon** (François Salignac de la Mothe), *Réfutation du système du P. Malebranche sur la nature et la grâce.* [Not published till 1820.]

1682   **Malebranche** (Nicolas), *Défense de l'Autheur de la Recherche de la Verité contre l'Accusation de M. de la Ville...* (Cologne: Guiljaume le Jeune).

1682   **Bayle** (Pierre), *Lettre à M. L. A. D. C. docteur de Sorbonne Ou il est prouvé par pleusieurs raisons tirées de la philosophie, e de la theologie, que les cometes ne sont point le presage d'aucun malheur* (Cologne: P. Marteau).

1683   **Malebranche** (Nicolas), *Méditations chréstiennes* ... (Cologne: d'Egmond). [OCM X]

1683   **Arnauld** (Antoine), *Des Vrayes et des fausses idées, contre ce qu'enseigne l'auteur de la Recherche de la vérité* (Clogne: Schouten).

1683   **Boussuet** (Jacques Benigne), *Oraison funebre de Marie-Therèse d'Autriche.* [See *Oevres de Bossuet*, edd. Velat (B.) & Champaillier (Y) (Paris: Pleiade, 1961)]

1684   **Malebranche** (Nicolas), *Réponse de l'auteur de la Recherche de la verité, au livre de Mr. Arnauld, des vrayes & des fausses Idées* (Rotterdam: Reinier Leers). [OCM VI]

1684   **Arnauld** (Antoine), *Défense de Mr Arnauld Docteur de Sorbonne, contre la réponse au livre des vraies et fausses idées* (Cologne: Nicolas Schouten).

1684   **Bayle** (Pierre), "Compte rendu du Traité de la nature et de la grâce", *Nouvelles de la république des lettres.*

1684   **Lamy** (Bernard), *Entretiens sur les sciences* (Bruxelles).

1684   **Leibniz** (G.W.), "Meditationes de cognitione, veritate et ideis", *Acta eruditorum.*

1684   **Ameline** (Claude), Traité de la volonté... (Paris: G. Desprez).

1684   **Jurieu** (Pierre), *L'Esprit de M. Arnaud* (Deventer: Jean Colombius).

1685   **Malebranche**, trans. L'Enfant (Jacob), *De inquirenda Veritate libri sex...Ex ultima editione Gallica...*(Geneva: Typis & sumptibus Societatis). [Reissued in 1687 (London: Abel Swalle).]

1685   **Arnauld** (Antoine), *Dissertation de Mr. Arnauld Docteur de Sorbonne, sur la maniere dont Dieu a fait les frequens miracles de l'ancienne loy par le ministere des anges. Pour servir de réponse aux nouvelles pensées de l'auteur du Traité de la nature & de la grâce dans un éclaircissement* [IV] (Cologne: Nicolas Schouten).

1685 (July)   **Malebranche** (Nicolas), *Réponse à une dissertation de Mr Arnauld contre un Eclaircissement du Traité de la Nature & de la Grâce. Dans laquelle on établit les principes nécessaires a l'intelligence de ce même Traité* (Rotterdam: Reinier Leers). [OCM VII]

1685	**Arnauld** (Antoine), *Réflexions philosophiques et théologiques sur le nouveau systeme de la nature & de la grâce. Livre I. Touchant l'ordre de la nature* (Cologne: Nicolas Schouten).
1685	**Malebranche** (Nicolas), *Trois lettres de l'auteur de la Recherche de la Verité touchant la Défense de Mr. Arnauld Contre la reponse au livre des vrayes & fausses Idées* (Rotterdam: Reinier Leers). [OCM VII]
[1686]	**Leibniz** (G.W.), 'petit discours de métaphysique'. Not published till the ninteenth century. Critical edition by Lestiènne (Henri) 1907 revised Robinet (André), *Discours de Métaphysique*, (Paris: Vrin, 1983).
1686	**Malebranche** (Nicolas), *Lettres du Pere Malebranche a un des ses Amis, Dans lesquelles il répond aux Reflexions Philosophiques & Théologiques de Mr Arnauld sur le Traité de la Nature & de la Grâce* (Rotterdam: Reinier Leers). [OCM VIII]
1686	**Arnauld** (Antoine), *Réflexions philosophiques et théologiques sur le nouveau systeme de la nature & de la grace. Livre II. Touchant l'ordre de la grace.* (Cologne: Nicolas Schouten).
1686	**Arnauld** (Antoine), *Réflexions philosophiques et théologiques sur le nouveau systeme de la nature & de la grace. Livre III. Touchant Jesus-Christ comme cause de la grace* (Cologne: Nicolas Schouten).
1686	**Bayle** (Pierre), *Réponse de l'auteur des Nouvelles de la République des Lettres, à l'avis qui lui a esté donné sur ce qu'il avait dit on faveur de P. Malebranche, touchant le plaisir des sens,* etc. (Rotterdam: de Grae).
1686	**Fontenelle** (Bernard le Bovier de) *Doutes sur le sistème physique des causes occasionelles.* (Rotterdam). [Ed. Depping (G-B.) *Oevres de Fontenelle.* Geneva: Slatkine Reprints, 1968.]
1687	**Malebranche** (Nicolas), *Deux Lettres du P Malebranche Prêtre de l'Oratoire, Touchant le II & le III Volume des Réflexions Philosophiques & Theologiques de Mr Arnauld* (Rotterdam: Reinier Leers). [OCD VIII]
1687	**Leibniz** (G.W.), "Lettre de M.L. sur un principe general utile à l'explication des loix de la nature par la consideration de la sagesse divine, pour servir de replique à la reponse du R.P.D. Malebranche", *Nouvelles de la république des lettres.*

134

1687   **Jurieu** (Pierre), *Traitté de la nature et de la grâce*. (Utrecht: Francois Halma).

1687   **Foucher** (Simon), *Dissertations sur la Recherche de la Vérité, contenant l'apologie des Académiciens, où l'on fait voir que leur maniere de philosopher est la plus conform au bon sens, pour servir de Réponse a la Critique de la Critique,...* (Paris: Estienne Michallet).

1687   **Bayle** (Pierre), *Dissertation sur le prétendu bonheur des plaisirs des sens, pour servir de réplique a la Réponse qu'a faite Mr. Bayle pour justifier ce qu'il a dit sur ce sujet dans ses Nouvelles de la République des Lettres...en faveur du P. Malebranche contre Mr Arnauld* (Cologne: N. Schouten).

1687   **Arnauld** (Antoine), *Dissertations sur le pretendu bonheur des sens* (Cologne: Nicolas Schouten).

1687   **Malebranche** (Nicolas), *Lettres du Pere Malebranche touchant celles de Mr Arnauld* (Rotterdam: Reinier Leers). [OCD VII]

1688   **Malebranche** (Nicolas), *Entretiens sur la Métaphysique et sur la Religion* (Rotterdam: Reinier Leers). [OCD XII]

1688   **Norris** (John), *The Theory and Regulation of Love* (Oxford: Henry Elements).

1689   **Norris** (John), *Reason and Religion: or the grounds and measures devotion consider'd from the nature of God* (London: Samuel Manship).

1690   **Régis** (Pierre-Sylvain), *Système de philosophie, contenant la logique, la métaphysique, la physique et la morale.* 3 vols. (Lyon: Thierry).

1690   **Locke** (John), *An Essay Concerning Human Understanding* (London: Holt).

1690   **Norris** (John), "Cursory Reflections upon a Book call'd An Essay concerning Human Understanding", appended to *Christian Blessedness...* (London: S. Manship).

1691   **Régis** (Pierre-Sylvain), *Cours entier de philosophie ou système general selon les principes de M. Descartes* (Amsterdam: Huguetan).

1692   **Malebranche** (Nicolas), *Des lois de la communication des mouvements...* (Paris: Pralard).

1692   **Abbadie** (Jacques), *L'art de se connaître soi-même ou la recherche des sources de la morale.* (Rotterdam: P. van der Slaart).

1693   **Malebranche** (Nicolas), *Réponse du P. Malebranche prestre de l'Oratoire a M. Régis* (Paris: Pralard).

[1693]   **Locke** (John), *An Examination of P. Malebranche's Opinion of Seeing All Things in God.* [Published posthumously in 1704, see below.]

1694   **Lelevel** (Henri), *La vraie et la fausse métaphysique où l'on réfute les sentiments de M. Regis et de ses adversairees sur cette matière. Avec plusieurs dissertations physiques et métaphysiques et toutes les pièces justificatives des sentiments du P. Malebranche par rapport à M. Regis* (Rotterdam: R. Leers).

1694   Trans. **Taylor** (Thomas), *Father Malebranche's Treatise concerning the Search after Truth. The whole work compleat. To Which is added the Author's Treatise of Nature and Grace...together with his answer to the animadversions upon the first volume: his defence against the accusations of Mr. De La Ville, &c., relating to the same subject.* 2 vols. (Oxford: Bennet).

[1694]   **Locke** (John), *Remarks on Some of Mr. Norris's Books wherein he asserts Pere Malebranche's Opinion, of our Seeing All Things in God.* [Published in *A Collection of Several Pieces of Mr. John Locke, never before published*, ed. P. DesMaixeaux (London: R. Franklin 1729).]

1694   Trans. **Sault** (Richard), *Malebranche's Search after Truth: or, a Treatise of the Nature of the Human Mind, and of its Management for avoiding Error in the Sciences. (To which is added the Author's defence against the accusations of Monsieur de la Ville. Also the life of...Malebranche...with...particulars of his controversie with...Arnauld...and Regis...Written by...Le Vasseur, etc.* 2 vols. (London: S. Manship).

1694-8   **Lamy** (F.J.), *De la connaissance de soi-même* (Paris: Pralard).

1695   **Norris** (John), *Letters concerning the Love of God, between the author of the Proposal to the Ladies* [Mary Astell], *and J. Norris; wherein his late discourse* [printed in vol 3 of 'Practical Discourses'], *shewing that it ought to be intire and exclusive of all other loves, is further cleared and justified* (London: S. Manship & R. Wilkin).

1695   Trans **anon.**, *Christian Conferences: Demonstrating the Truth of the Christian Religion and Morality. By F. Malebranche. To which is*

136

added, *his Meditations on Humility and Repentance* (London: J. Whitlock).

1695 Trans **anon.**, *A Treatise of Nature and Grace . [By Malebranche] To which is added the author's idea of Providence; and his answers to several objections against the foregoing discourse* (London: J. Whitlock).

1695 [**Abbadie,** Jacques], *The Art of Knowing One-self: or, an Enquiry into the Sources of morality. Written originally in French* (Oxford: Clements and Howell).

1696 **Malebranche** (Nicolas), *Entretiens sur la Métaphysique et sur la Religion. Nouvelle Edition, revué, corrigée, & augmentée de plusieurs Entretiens sur la Mort* (Paris: Reinier Louis Roulland). [OED XII-XIII]

1696 **Masham** (Damaris), *A Discourse concerning the Love of God* (London: A. & J. Churchill).

1697 **Sergeant** (John), *Solid Philosophy asserted, against the Fancies of the Ideists ...* (London: Roger Clavil & others).

1698 **Fardella** (A.), *Animae humanae natura ab Augustino detecta* (Venice).

1699 **Lamy** (F.J.), *Lettres de R. P. Lamy...pour répondre a la critique du R.P. Malebranche sur les trois derniers éclaircissements de la "Connaissance de soi-même" touchant l'amour désintéressé.*

1699 Trans. **Shipton** (James), *A Treatise of Morality...written in French by F. Malebranche...* 2 vols. (London: J. Knapton).

1699 **Lowde** (James), *Moral Essays: Wherein some of Mr. Locke's and Monsir. Malebranche's Opinions are Briefly examin'd* (London: Thos Bennet & York: Hildyard).

1699 **Faydit** (Pierre-Valentin), *Lettres théologiques sur les nouvelles opinions du temps...Première lettre: La presbytéromachie, ou le combat des deux fameux prêtres, inventeurs de nouvelle doctrine, Michel de Molinos et Louis de Mallebranche (sic), prêtre de l'Oratoire, s'entre détruisants l'un l'autre par leurs principes.*

1699 **Malebranche** (Nicolas), *Réflexions sur la lumière et les couleurs et la generation du feu. (Memoires de l'Academie des Sciences).*

1700	Trans. **Taylor** (Thomas), *Father Malebranche his treatise concerning the Search after Truth... To which is added the author's treatise of Nature and Grace...The second edition, corrected...With the addition of a Short Discourse upon Light and Colours, etc.* 3 pt. (London: Bennet, Leigh and Midwinter).
1701-4	**Norris** (John), *An Essay Towards the Theory of the Ideal or Intelligible World.* 2 Parts. (London: S. Manship).
1704	**Taylor** (Thomas), *Two Covenants of God with Mankind...in an Essay designed to shew the Use and Advantage of some of Mr. Malebranche's Principles in the Theories of Providence and Grace* (London: Tho. Bennet).
1704	**Malebranche** (Nicolas), *Réponse du Pere Malebranche prêtre de l'Oratoire a la troisieme lettre de M. Arnauld docteur de Sorbonne touchant les Idées & les Plaisirs* (Amsterdam: Henry Westein). [OCM IX].
1704	**Trevisano** (Bernardo), *Meditazioni filosofiche* (Venezia).
1705	**Astell** (Mary), *The Christian Religion, as profess'd by a Daughter of the Church of England* (London: R. Wilkin).
1706	**Locke** (John), "An Examination of P. Malebranche's Opinion of Our Seeing All Things in God." In ed. King (P) *Posthumous Works of Mr John Locke.* (London:
[1707]	**Leibniz** (G.W.), Comments on Locke's "Examination" [Not published till much later]. See A. Robinet (ed.) *Malebranche et Leibniz*, pp. 395ff.
1708	**Malebranche** (Nicolas), *Entretien d'un philosophe chrétien et d'un philosophe chinois* (Paris: David). [OCM XV]
1708	**[Marquer**, Louis, S.J.], *Avis touchant l'entretien d'un philosophe Chrétien...inserées dans les Memoires de Trévoux du mois de Juillet 1708* (Paris: Michel David) OCM XV 63-76.
1709	**Basselin** (R.), *Dissertation sur l'origine des idées où l'on fait voir contre M. Descartes, le R.P. Malebranche et Messieurs de Port-Royal, qu'elles nous viennent toutes des sens et comment* (Paris: Delauine).
1709	**Vico** (Giambattista), *De Antiquissima Italorum Sapientia* (Neapoli).

138

1710   **Leibniz** (G.W.), *Essais de Theodicée sur la bonté de Dieu, la liberté de l'homme et l'origine du mal* (Amsterdam: I. Troyel).

1710   **Berkeley** (George), *A Treatise Concerning the Principles of Human Knowledge, Part I. Wherein the chief Causes of Error and Difficulty in the Sciences, with the Grounds of Scepticism, Atheism, and Irreligion, are inquir'd into* (Dublin: Jeremy Pepyat).

[1712]   **Leibniz** (G.W.), *Entretien de Philarete et d'Ariste, suite de premier entretien d'Ariste et de Theodore* [published in C.I. Gerhardt (ed.), *G.W. Leibniz: Die Philosophischen Schriften* (Berlin, 1885), Vol. 6: 579-594].

1713   **Collier** (Arthur), *Clavis Universalis: or, a New inquiry after truth. Being a demonstration of the non-existence, or the impossibility of an external world* (London: Robert Gosling).

1713   **Fénelon** (Francois Salignac de la Mothe), *Demonstration de l'existence de Dieu* (Amsterdam: F. l'Honoré).

1713-14   "Correspondance de Malebranche et de Mairan", first edited by V. Cousin and published in *Fragments de philosophie cartésienne* (Paris: Charpentier, 1845).

1713   **Boursier** (Abbé Laurent-Francois), *De l'Action de Dieu sur les créatures, où l'on prouve la prémotion physique par le resonnement et où l'on examine plusieurs questions qu on rapport a la nature des esprits et a la grace* (Paris: Babuty).

1715   **Malebranche** (Nicolas), *Réflexions sur la Prémotion physique* (Paris: Michel David). [OCM XVI]

1715   **Du Terte** (Rudolphe), *Réfutation d'un nouveau systeme de métaphysique proposé par le Pere Malebranche.* (Paris: Raymond Mazieres).

[1715 (Nov)] **Leibniz** (G.W.), Remarks on Du Tertre's *Réfutation* in a letter to Nicolas Remond. [Published in A. Robinet (ed.) *Malebranche et Leibniz*, pp. 478ff.]

[1715-6]   **Leibniz** (G.W.), Incomplete when Leibniz died. Translated by Henry Rosemount, Jr. and Daniel J. Cook as *Discourse on the Natural Theology of the Chinese* (University of Hawaii Press 1977).

1716   **Fontenelle** (Bernard le Buvier de) Éloge du P. Malebranche. See OCM XIX 999-1012.

(B)	THE EIGHTEENTH CENTURY RECEPTION OF MALEBRANCHE: A SELECTION OF MALEBRANCHE-RELATED WRITINGS (1720-1800)

1720   **Anon.**, *L'âme matérialle.* New edition with notes and introduction by Alain Niderst (Paris: P.U.F., 1973).

[c1720]   **André** (Yves Marie), *La Vie du R. P. Malebranche prêtre de l'Oratoire avec l'Histoire de ses Ouvrages.* [First published 1886. Reprinted 1970, Geneva: Slatkine Reprints]

1721   **Montesquieu** (Charles Louis de Secondat, Baron de), *Lettres Persanes* (Cologne).

1724   **Buffier** (Claude, S.J.), *Traité des premières vérités...* (Paris: la veuve Mauge).

1724   **Buffier** (Claude, S.J.), *Observations sur la métaphysique du P. Malebranche* (Paris).

1725   **Vico** (Giambattista), *Principi di una Scienza Nuova...* (Neapoli).

1728   **Stolius** (G.), *Introductio in historiam litterariam...* (Iena: Meyer), Vol. 2, Ch. 2 & Vol. 3, Ch. 1.

1733   **Hardouin** (Jean, S.J.), *Athei detecti* (Amsterdam: du Sauzet).

1733   **Prévost** (A.F.), *Le pour et le contre, ouvrage periodique du gout nouveau* (Paris: Didot).

1739   **Hume** (David), *A treatise of human nature : being an attempt to introduce the experimental method of reasoning into moral subjects* (London: John Noon).

1741   **André** (Yves Marie), *Essai sur le beau...* (Paris: H.L. & J. Guerin).

1746   **Condillac** (Étienne Bonnot de), *Traité de systèmes, où l'on en démèle les inconvenients et les advantages* (Amsterdam and Leipzig), Ch. VII.

1747   **Gerdil** (Giacinto Sigismondo), *L'Immaterialité de l'âme demontrée contre M. Locke...* (Turin: Imprimerie Royale).

1748   **Montesquieu** (Charles Louis de Secondat, Baron de), *De l'Esprit des lois* (Geneva: J.S. Vernet), I.I.

1748   **Gerdil** (Giacinto Sigismondo), *Défence du sentiment du P. Malebranche sur la nature, & l'origine des Idées contre l'Examen de M. Locke par le P. Gerdil Barnabite...* (Turin: Imprimerie Royale).

1748   **Hume** (David), *Philosophical Essays concerning Human Understanding* (London: A. Millar).

1751   **Hume** (David), *Enquiry concerning the Principles of Morals* (London).

1753   **Lelarge de Lignac** (Abbé Joseph-Adrien), *Élemens de métaphysique tirés de l'experience ou Lettres à un matérialiste sur la nature de l'âme.* (Paris: Dasaint et Saillant).

1753   **Bouillier** (D.R.), *Apologie de la métaphysique, à l'occasion du "Discours préliminaire" de l'"Encyclopédie"...* (Amsterdam: Catuffe).

1758   **Gerdil** (Giacinto Sigismondo), *Histoires des sectes des philosophes* (Paris).

1758   **Helvétius** (Claude Adrien), *De l'Esprit* (Paris: Durard), Discours 1, Ch. 1, Discours 3, Ch. 9.

1759   **Carracioli** (L.A.), *La conversation avec soi-même* (Lieges: Bassompièrre).

1759   **Roche** (Λ.M.), *Traité de la nature de l'âme et de l'origine de ses coinnaissances, contre le système de M. Locke et ses partisans* (Paris: Lottin).

1761   **Keranflech** (Charles Hercule de), *Hypothèse des petits tourbillons...* (Rennes: Vatar et fils).

1761   **Rousseau** (Jean-Jacques), *Julie, ou la Nouvelle Heloise* (Amsterdam).

1762   **Rousseau** (Jean-Jacques), "Profession du foi du vicaire savoyard", in *Émile, ou del' Éducation* (Amsterdam).

1764   **Voltaire** (François-Marie Arouet de), *Dictionnaire philosophique, ou la raison par alphabet* (Geneva, falsely imprinted as "Londres").

1764 posth.   **Meslier** (Jean), "Testament de Jean Meslier", in Voltaire, *L'évangile de la raison...* (Amsterdam: M.M. Rey, falsely imprinted as "Londres: aux depens de la Compagnie de Jesus").

1764   **Reid** (Thomas), *An Inquiry into the Human Mind on the Principles of Common Sense* (Edinburgh), Ch. 1.

1765   **Keranflech** (Charles Hercule de), *Essai sur la raison* (Paris: Vatar).

1768   **Naigeon** (Jacques André), *Le militaire philosophe; ou, Difficultés sur la religion proposées au R.P. Malebranche...par un ancien officier* (London). [Abridged by Naigeon with a contribution from Holbach.]

1768   **Keranflech** (Charles Hercule de), *Suite de "l'Essai sur la raison"* (Rennes: Vatar et fils).

1769   (**Voltaire**, Francois-Marie Arouet de), "Tout en Dieu. Commentaire sur Malebranche par l'abbé de Tilladet."

1772   **Keranflech** (Charles Hercule de), *Dissertation sur les miracles, pour servir d'éclaircissement au sistème de l'impuissance des causes serandes* (Rennes: J.C. Vatar).

1772   **Holbach** (Paul Heinrich Dietrich, Baron d'), *le bon sens, ou Idées naturelles opposées aux idées surnaturelles* (Londres

1773 posth.   **Helvétius** (Claude Adrien), *De l'Homme* (Londres: Sociétié typographique).

1773   **Holbach** (Paul Heinrich Dietrich, Baron d'), *Système social...* (Amsterdam, falsely imprinted 'Londres').

1776   **Holbach** (Paul Heinrich Dietrich, Baron d'), *La morale universelle...* (Amsterdam).

1780   **Buffier** (Claude), *First Truths and the Origin of our Opinions Explained* (London: J. Johnson). Trans. of Buffier's *Traité des premières verités* (1724).

1780   **Hennert** (J.F.), "Het Spinozisme vergeleken met de gewelens van Malebranche", in *Uitgeleezene Verhandelingen over Wijsbegeerte en Fraage Lettern* (Utrecht).

1785   **Reid** (Thomas), *Essay on the Intellectual Powers of Man* (Edinburgh) Ch. 7.

1785   **Keranflech** (Charles Hercule de), *L'idée de l'ordre surnaturel* (Rennes: Vatar).

1797   **Tiedemann** (D.) *Geist der speculativen Philosophie* (Marburg), Vol. 6: 157-203.

(C)   **MODERN EDITIONS OF MALEBRANCHE**

Critical edition of texts

Dir. **Robinet** (André) (1958-67) *Oevres complètes de* Malebranche. Paris: Vrin.

Volume contents:

I-III	*Recherche de la vérité (& Éclaircissements).*
IV	*Conversations chrétiennes*
V	*Traité de la nature et de la grâce*
VI-IX	*Recueil de toutes les reponses à M. Arnauld*
X	*Meditations chrestiennes et métaphysiques*
XI	*Traité de Morale*
XII	*Entretiens sur la métaphysique et sur la religion*
XIII	*Entretiens sur la mort*
XIV	*Traité de l'amour de Dieu et lettres au P. Lamy*
XV	*Entretien d'un philosophe crétien et d'un philosophe chinois*
XVI	*Réflexions sur la prémotion physique*
XVII-1	*Pièces jointes et Écrits divers*
XVII-2	*Mathematica*

XVIII   *Correspondance et actes (1638-1689)*

XIX   *Correspondance et actes (1690-1715)*

XX   *Documents biographiques et bibliographiques. Index des citations,
            bibliques, patristiques, philosophiques, et scientifiques*

Modern English translations

Trans. Doney (Willis), *Dialogues on Metaphysics* (New York: Abaris Books, 1980)

Trans. Ginsberg (Morris), *Dialogues on Metaphysics and Religion* (London: Allen &
        Unwin, 1923).

Trans. Iorio (Dominick A.), *Nicolas Malebranche: Dialogue Between a Christian
        Philosopher and a Chinese Philosopher on the Existence and Nature
        of God* (Washington, D.C.: University Press of America, 1980).

Trans. Lennon (T.M.) and Olscamp (P.J.), *The Search After Truth* (Columbus, Ohio:
        Ohio State U. P., 1980).

Trans. Riley (Patrick) *Nicolas Malebranche: Treatise of Nature and Grace* (Oxford
        University Press, forthcoming 1991).

II.   SELECT BIBLIOGRAPHY OF SECONDARY WRITINGS
         RELATED TO MALEBRANCHE: HIS CRITICS AND HIS
         SUCCESSORS

(A)   **MALEBRANCHE AND HIS CONTEMPORARIES**

144

Bouillier (Francisque), *Mémoire sur la vision en Dieu de Malebranche* (Orleans: Caignet-Darnault, 1852).

Bouillier (Francisque), *Histoire de la philosophie cartésienne* (Paris: Durand, 1854), II. Chs. XVI-XX.

Ch. XVI discusses Malebranche's critics (including Foucher, Faydit, Du Tertre, Hardouin and Voltaire). There is substantial discussion of Leibniz and Bayle.

Damiron (Jean Philibert), *Essai sur l'histoire de la philosophie en France au XVIIe siècle* (Paris: Machette, 1846) 2: 352-596.

Account of Malebranche's main controversies, including Bossuet, Boursier, Fénelon and F. Lamy.

Labbas (L.), *La grace et la liberté dans Malebranche* (Paris: Vrin, 1931).

Montcheuil (Yves de, S.J.), *Malebranche et le quietisme* (Paris: Aubier, 1946).

Particular attention to Malebranche's relations with F. Lamy, Bossuet and Fénelon.

Ollé-Laprune (L.), *La philosophie de Malbranche* (Paris: Ladrange, 1870) Vol. II.

Ch. I "Les critiques de Malebranche" gives particular attention to Locke, Fénelon, the Jesuits, Bayle, Dortous de Mairan and Leibniz. Ch. II "Les disciples de Malebranche" includes sections on François Lamy, Boursier and André as well as the more faithful but less original disciples such as Bernard Lamy, Lanion and Lelevel.

Pillon (François), "Malebranche et ses critiques", *Année philosophique 4* (1893) : 109-206.

Riley (Patrick), *The General Will Before Rousseau: The Transformation of the Divine into the Civic* (Princeton: Princeton U.P. 1986), esp. Chs. I-III.

The most comprehensive account available in English of the controversies provoked by Malebranche's *Traité de la Nature et de la Grâce*.

FOUCHER Simon, (1644-96)

Buchenau (Arthur), 'Über Malebranches Lehre von der Wahrheit und ihre Bedeutung für die Methodik der Wissenschaften', *Archiv für die Geschichte der Philosophie* 16 (1910): 145-184.

Gouhier (Henri), "Le première polemique de Malebranche", *Revue d'histoire de la philosophie et d'histoire generale de la civilisation 1* (1927): 23-48, 68-191.

Rabbe (F.), *Étude philosophique. L'abbé Simon Foucher, Chanoine de la Sainte-Chapelle de Dijon* (Paris: Didier, 1867) 36-86.

Watson (Richard A.), "The breakdown of Cartesian metaphysics", *Journal of the History of Philosophy* 1 (1964): 177-197.

Watson (Richard A.), *The Downfall of Cartesianism, 1673-1712, A Study of Epistemological Issues in Late 17th Century Cartesianism* (The Hague: Nijhoff, 1966).

Watson (Richard A.), "Simon Foucher" in Paul Edwards (ed.), *Encyclopedia of Philosophy* (New York: Macmillan, 1967), Vol. 3.

Watson (Richard A.), Introduction to a reprint of Foucher's *Critique de la Recherche de la Vérité* (New York: Johnson Reprint, 1969).

Watson (Richard A.), *The Breakdown of Cartesian Metaphysics* (Atlantic Highlands, NJ: Humanities Press Intl., 1987).

DESGABETS, Dom Robert (1600-1678)

Lemaire (P.), *Le cartésianisme chez les Benedictins. Dom Robert Desgabets, son système, son influence, et son école, d'après pleusieurs manuscrits et des documents rares ou inédits* (Paris: Alcan, 1901), Ch. 7.

Prost (Joseph), *Essai sur l'atomisme et l'occasionalisme dans la philosophie cartésienne* (Paris: Paulin, 1907).

Robinet (André), "Dom Robert Desgabets. Le conflit philosophique avec Malebranche et l'oeuvre de la science", *Revue de synthèse* 95 (1974): 65-83.

See also under "Foucher" above.

DE LA VILLE, Louis, nom de plume of L. Le Valois, S.J. (1639-1700).

Gouhier (Henri), "Philosophie chrétienne et théologie. A propos de la seconde polemique de Malebranche", *Revue philosophique de la France et de l'étranger* 125 (1938): 151-193.

See also under "Jesuits" below.

FÉNELON, Francois de Salignac de la Mothe (1651-1715)

Brunschwicg (Léon), "Malebranche et Fénelon", in *Le progrès de la conscience dans la philosophie occidentale* (Paris: Alcan, 1927), vol. 1, 195-222.

Daniel (Charles), "De l' optimisme en philosophie et en théologie", *Études de Théologie, de Philosophie et d'Histoire* N S I (1859): 384-436.

Desautels (A.R.), "Fénelon critique de Malebranche. En marge de 'Malebranche et le quietisme' du P. de Montscheuil." *Revue thomiste* 53, 2 (1953): 347-66. See also *Bouiller* (1852), *Damiron* and *Monscheuil* Ch. I above, and *Bracken* 1965, Chs 1-2 below.

BAYLE, Pierre (1647-1706)

Robinet (André), "La philosophie de P. Bayle devant les philosophies de Malebranche et de Leibniz", in Paul Dibon (ed.), *Pierre Bayle, le philosophe de Rotterdam* (Institut Français d'Amsterdam, Maison Descartes, 1959), 48-65.

See also *Bouillier* 1854 Vol. II, Ch. XX and *Riley* 93-98.

ARNAULD, Antoine (1612-94)

Brun (Marcell), "Un aspect de la théologie de Malebranche: Le Christ cause occasionelle de la grâce", *Doctor communis* 5 (1952), 80-115.

Church (R.W.), *A Study in the Philosophy of Malebranche* (London: Allen & Unwin, 1931, reissued Port Washington, N.Y.: Kennikat Press, 1970).

Cook (Monte), "Acts and Objects: Malebranche and Arnauld on Ideas", Ph.D. Thesis (University of Iowa, 1971).

Cook (Monte), "Arnauld's alleged representationalism", *Journal of the History of Philosophy* 12 (1972): 53-62.

Delbos (Victor), "La controverse d'Arnauld et de Malebranche sur la nature et l'origin des idées", in *Étude de la philosophie de Malebranche* (Paris: Vrin, 1924).

Glauser (Richard), "Arnauld critique de Malebranche: le statut des idées", *Revue de Théologie et de Philosophie* 120 (1988): 390-410.

Kremer (E.J.), "Malebranche and Arnauld: the Controversy over the Nature of Ideas", Ph.D. Thesis (Yale, 1961).

Lewis (Geneviève), "L'intervention de Nicole dans la polémique entre Arnauld et Malebranche d'après des lettres inédites", *Revue philosophique de la France et de l'étranger* 75 (1950): 483-506.

Lennon (Thomas M.) "The Controversy with Arnauld", a section of the commentary appended to the 1980 English translation of *The Search after Truth* (see under "Translations" above), 793-809.

Lovejoy (A.C.), "'Representative ideas' in Malebranche and Arnauld", *Mind*, 32 (1923) : 449-461.

Luciano (P.), *Expozitione critica della controversia tra N. Malebranche et A. Arnauld intorno alla natura e all'origine delle idee* (Torino, 1867).

Marzorati (Filippo), "La critica di Arnauld alla ideologia di Malebranche", *Revista di filosofia neoscolastica* (1914).

Nadler (Steven M.), *Arnauld and the Cartesian Philosophy of Ideas* (Manchester: Manchester U.P., 1989).

Radner (Daisie), " Representationalism in Arnauld's act theory of perception", *Journal of the History of Philosophy* 14 (1976): 96-98.

Wahl (Russell), "The Arnauld-Malebranche controversy and Descartes' ideas", *Monist* 71 (1988): 560-572.

See also *Labbas* above and OCM VI-IX.

BOSSUET, Jacques-Benigne (1627-1704)

See *Bouillier* 1852, *Brunschwicg, Damiron, Labbas* and *Monscheuil* above.

LAMY, Bernard (1640-1715)

Girbal, (F.), "A propos de Malebranche et de Bernard Lamy", *Revue internationale de philosophie* 9 (1955): 288-290.

Girbal (F.), *Bernard Lamy (1640-1715), Étude bio-bibliographique avec des textes inédites* (Paris: P.U.F., 1964).

See also under "Other Oratorians" below.

OTHER ORATORIANS

Batterel (Louis), ed. A. M-P Ingold et E. Bonnardet, *Memoires pour servir a l'histoire de l'Oratoire* (Paris: Picard, 4 vols., 1902-05), Vol. 4. Chapters on Malebranche (pp. 323-365) and Bernard Lamy (pp. 365-408).

Robinet (André), "Le groupe malebranchiste de l'Oratoire" in *Malebranche Vivant*, OCM XX 137-140.

LEIBNIZ, G.W. (1646-1716).

Boutroux (Emile), *La philosophie allemande au XVIIe siècle, Les predecesseurs de Leibniz* (Paris: Vrin, 1929, reprinted 1948) 42-52.

Brown (Stuart), *Leibniz* (Brighton: Harvester, 1984) Ch. 7.

Brown (Stuart), *Introduction to G.W. Leibniz: Discourse on Metaphysics and Related Writings*, ed. & trans. (R. Niall D.) Martin & (Stuart) Brown (Manchester: Manchester University Press, 1988).

Buchenau (Arthur), "Zur Geschichte de Briefwechsels zwischen Leibniz und Malebranche", *Archiv für die Geschichte der Philosophie* 18 (1905) 315-321.

Jolley (Nicholas), "Leibniz and Malebranche on innate ideas", *Philosophical Review* 97 (1988): 71-91.

Jolley (Nicholas), *The Light of the Soul: Theories of Ideas in Leibniz, Malebranche, and Descartes* (Oxford: Clarendon Press, 1990).

Loemker (Leroy E.), "A note on the origin and problem of Leibniz's discourse of 1686", *Journal of the History of Ideas*, 8 (1947): 449-466.

Mouy (Paul), *Les loix du choc d'après Malebranche* (Paris: Vrin, 1927).

Mouy (Paul), *Le développement de la physique cartésienne: 1646-1712* (Paris: Vrin, 1934), Ch. 4.

Mungello (David E.), "Malebranche and Chinese philosophy", *Journal of the History of Ideas* 41 (1980) 551-578.

Naert (Émilienne), *Leibniz et la querelle du pur amour* (Paris: Vrin, 1959).

Robinet (André) ed., *Malebranche et Leibniz. Relations personelles, présentées avec les textes complets des auteurs et de leurs correspondents, revus, corrigés et inédits* (Paris: Vrin, 1955).

Robinet (André), "Malebranche et Leibniz a l'Ordinattur: de 'Pim 71 à Monado 72'‹, *Revue Internationale de Philosophie* 27 (1973): 49-65.

Siwek (Paul), " Optimism in philosophy", *New Scholasticism* 22 (1948): 417-439.

Sleigh (Robert C., Jr.), "Leibniz on Malebranche on Causality", in edd. Jan Cover and Mark Kulstad, *Central Themes in Early Modern Philosophy: Essays Presented to Jonathan Bennett* (Indianapolis: Hackett, 1990).

Stieler (Georg), *Leibniz und Malebranche und das Theodizeeproblem* (Darmstadt: Reichl, 1930).

Weissmann (G.), *L'influenza del Malebranche sulla filosofia del Leibniz* (Innsbruck: Wagner, 1895).

Woolhouse (Roger S.), "Leibniz and occasionalism", in ed. R.S. Woolhouse, *Metaphysics and the Philosophy of Science in the Seventeenth and Eighteenth Centuries* (Dordrecht: Kluwer Academic, 1988).

See also *Bouillier* 1854 above, Vol. II, Chs. XVIII-XIX, and *Watson* 1987 above.

FONTENELLE, Bernard Le Bovier de (1657-1757)

Robinet (André), "Malebranche dans la pensée de Fontenelle", *Revue de Synthèse* 82 (1961) III, 21: 79-86.

Spener (E.M.A.), "Malebranches Okkasionalismus im Licht der Kritik Fontenelles", *Archiv für Geschichte der Philosophie* 29 (1916) 256-280.

RÉGIS, Pierre-Sylvain (1632-1707)

Smith (Norman Kemp), "Malebranche's theory of the perception of distance and magnitude", *British Journal of Psychology* 1 (1905): 191-204.

LAMY, Francois (1636-1711)

Henry (Charles), "Une critique de Malebranche par le Benedictin Dom F. Lami", *Annales de philosophie chrétienne* 6, 96 (1879): 340-347.

See also *Damiron, Monscheuil* Ch. I and *Ollé-Laprune* above, as well as OCM XIV.

DE MAIRAN, J. J. Dortous (1678-1771)

Getchev (George S.), "Some of Malebranche's reactions to Spinoza revealed in his correspondence with Dortous de Mairan", *Philosophical Review* XLI, 4 (1932): 385-394.

Pillon (F.), "L'évolution de l'idéalisme au XVII siècle, Spinozisme et Malebranchisme. La correpondance de Mairan et de Malebranche", *Année Philosophique* 5 (1894): 85-199.

JESUITS (including André, Marquer, Boursier & Du Tertre).

Allard (Emmy), *Die Angriffe gegen Descartes und Malebranche im Journal de Trévoux*, 1701-1715 (Halles: Niemeyer, 1914).

Sortais (Gaston, S.J.), "Le cartésianisme chez les Jesuites francais au XVIIe et au XVIIe siecle", *Archives de philosophie* 6 13 (1929), Ch. 4.

Robinet (André), "Malebranche et les Jesuits", in *Malebranche vivant. OCM* XX: 205-224.

See also under "De Ville". See *Bouillier 1852, Damiron* and *Labbas* above.

(B) MALEBRANCHE AND EIGHTEENTH CENTURY FRENCH PHILOSOPHY

Acworth (Richard), "Malebranche and his heirs", *Journal of the History of Ideas* 38 (1977): 673-676.

Contrasts Malebranche's reception in France and England.

Alquié (Ferdinand), *Le Cartésianisme de Malebranche* (Paris: Vrin, 1974).

An important treatment of Malebranche and his influence on later philosophy, especially in France.

Deprun (Jean), *La philosophie de l'inquiétude en France au XVIIIe siecle* (Paris: Vrin, 1979).

Riley (Patrick), *The General Will Before Rousseau: The Transformation of the Divine into the Civic* (Princeton: Princeton U.P. 1986).

Separate chapters on Montesquieu and Rousseau.

Robinet (André), "L'attitude politique de Malebranche", *Le XVIIe siecle* 38 (1958): 1-27.

MESLIER, Jean (1678-1733)

Deprun (Jean), "Meslier et l'heritage scolastique", *Études sur le Curé Meslier* (Aix-en-Provence, 1964).

QUESNAY, François (1684-1774)

Schuhl (Pierre Maxime), "Malebranche et Quesnay", *Revue philosophique de la France et de l'étranger* 125 (1938): 313-315.

MONTESQUIEU, Charles Louis de Secondat, Baron de (1689-1707)

Beyer (Charles Jacques), "Montesquieu et la philosophie de l'ordre", in *Studies on Voltaire and the 18th century* 87 (1972) 145-166.

See also *Riley* Ch. 4, *Robinet* 24-7.

VOLTAIRE, François-Marie Arouet de (1694-1778)

Deprun (Jean), "Le Dictionairre philosophique et Malebranche", *Annales de la Faculté des Lettres*, N S 50 (1965) : 73-78.

PRÉVOST, Abbé A.F.

Deprun (Jean), "Themes malebranchistes dans l'oevre de Prévost", *Annales de la Faculté des Lettres*, N S 50 (1965): 155-172.

LELARGE, Joseph-Adrièn, Abbé de Lignac (c.1700-1762)

Ollé-Laprune (L.), *La philosophie de Malebranche* (Paris: Ladrange, 1870), II : 209-217.

See also *Azouvi* below.

BRUNET, Claude (fl. 1703-1717)

Larguier des Bancels (J.), "Sur un Malebranchiste peu connu", *Revue philosophique de la france et de l'étranger* 141, 4 (1951), 566.

ROUSSEAU, Jean-Jacques (1712-1778)

152

Bréhier (Emile), "Les Lectures malebranchistes de Jean-Jacques Rousseau", *Revue internationale de philosophie* 1 (1938): 98-120. (Paris: P.U.F.).

Dugas (L.), 'Rousseau et Malebranche', *Revue pedagogique* NS 72 (1918): 79-99.

Postigliola (Alberto), "De Malebranche a Rousseau: Les Apories de la volonté générale et la revanche du 'raisonneur violent'", *Annales de la Société Jean-Jacques Rousseau* 39 (1980).

Riley (Patrick), "The general will before Rousseau", *Political Theory* 6 (1978): 485-516.

Robinet (André), "A propos d'ordre dans la Profession de foi du vicaire savoyard", *Studi filosofici* 1 (1978).

See also *Riley*, Ch. 5.

CONDILLAC, Etiènne Bonnot de (1715-1780)

Azouvi (François), "Genese du temps propre chez Malebranche, Condillac, Lelarge De Lignac et Maine de Biran", *Archives de Philosophie* 45 (1982): 85-107.

KERANFLECH, Charles Hercule de (1730-)

Bouillier (Francisque), *Histoire de la philosophie cartésienne* (Paris: Durand, 1854), II, Ch. XXVI.

Rodis-Lewis (Geneviève), "Un malebranchiste meconnu: Keranflech", *Revue philosophique* 89, 1 (1964): 21-28.

CONDILLAC, Etiènne Bonnot de (1715-1780)

McNiven Hine (Ellen), *A Critical Study of Condillac's* Traité des Systèmes (The Hague: Hijhoff, 1979).

(C) MALEBRANCHE AND BRITISH PHILOSOPHY FROM LOCKE AND NORRIS TO HUME

GENERAL

Acworth (Richard), "Malebranche and his heirs", *Journal of the History of Ideas* 38 (1977): 673-676.

Contrasts Malebranche's reception in France and England, with particular attention to Norris.

Lennon (Thomas M.), "Representationalism, judgment and perception of distance: further to Yolton and McCrae", *Dialogue* 19 (1980: 151-162.

Lyon (Georges Henri Joseph), *L'idealisme en Angleterre au XVIIe siècle* (Paris: Alcan, 1888).

> Gives an account of Malebranche's English "prosélytes": Norris, Taylor and Collier. Special attention to Berkeley.

McCracken (Charles J.), *Malebranche and British Philosophy* (Oxford: Clarendon Press, 1983)

> This important study contains chapters on the English Malebrancheans (including Norris, Taylor and Collier), Locke, Berkeley, Hume, Reid and "Malebranche in Colonial America" (including Samuel Johnson and Jonathan Edwards).

Muirhead (John H.), *The Platonic Tradition in Anglo-Saxon Philosophy* (London: George Allen & Unwin).

> Discusses the connection between Malebranche's philosophy and those of Norris and Collier.

Norton (David Fate), "The myth of 'British Empiricism'", *History of European Ideas* 1 (1981): 331-344.

Yolton (John W.), "Ideas and knowledge in seventeenth century philosophy", *Journal of the History of Philosophy* 13 (1975): 145-165.

LOCKE, John (1632-1704)

Acworth (Richard), "Locke's First Reply to John Norris", *Locke Newsletter* (1971).

Johnston (Charlotte), "Locke's Examination of Malebranche and John Norris", *Journal of the History of Ideas* 19 (1958): 553-4.

Matthews (H.E.), "Locke, Malebranche and the Representative Theory", *Locke Newsletter* (1971): 12-21, reprinted in ed. Ian Tipton, *Locke on Human Understanding* (Oxford: Oxford U. P., 1977).

Yolton (John W.), "Representation and realism: some reflections on the way of ideas", *Mind* 76 (1987): 318-330.

> See also *Lennon* above.

NORRIS, John (1659-1712)

Acworth (R.), *La philosophie de John Norris 1657-1712* (Lille-Paris: Champion, 1973), trans. *The Philosophy of John Norris of Bemerton, 1657-1712* (Hildesheim: Olms, 1973).

Acworth (R.), "La disparation de la matiere chez les malebranchistes anglais J. Norris et A. Collier" in ed. *Jean-Luc Marion, La passion de la raision. Hommage à Ferdinand Alquié* (Paris: P.U.F., 1983).

See also *Acworth, Muirhead, McCracken* and *Lyon* above.

BERKELEY, George (1685-1753)

Bracken (Harry M.), "Berkeley and Malebranche on ideas", *Modern Schoolman* 41 (1963): 1-15.

Bracken (Harry M.), *The Early Reception of Berkeley's Immaterialism: 1710-1733* (Den Haag: Nijhoff, rev. edition 1965).

Bracken (Harry M.), *Berkeley* (London: MacMillan, 1974): Ch. 12.

Brykman (Geneviève), "Berkeley: sa lecture de Malebranche a travers de Dictionnaire de Bayle", *Revue internationale de philosophie* 114 (1975): 496-514.

Fritz (Anita D.), "Malebranche and the Immaterialism of Berkeley", *Review of Metaphysics* 3 (1949): 59-80.

Fritz (Anita D.), "Berkeley's Self: Its Origin in Malebranche", *Journal of the History of Ideas* 5 (1954): 554-72.

Fritz (Anita D.), "An Estimate of the Influence of Malebranche upon the Philosophy of Berkeley", Ph.D. Thesis (Bryn Mawr, 1958).

Gueroult (Martial), *Berkeley; quatre études sur la perception et sur Dieu* (Paris: Aubier, 1956).

Gueroult (Martial), "Dieu et la grammaire de la nature selon George Berkeley", *Revue de théologie et de philosophie* 3 (1954): 244-265.

Immerwahr (John), "Berkeley's causal thesis", *New Scholasticism* 48 (1974): 153-170.

Jessop (T.E.), "Malebranche and Berkeley", *Revue internationale de philosophie* 1 (1938): 121-42.

Leroux (Emannuel), "Note concernant l'influence de Malebranche sur Berkeley", *Revue de métaphysique et de morale* 45 (1938): 437-448.

Luce (A.A.), *Berkeley and Malebranche. A study in the origin of Berkeley's thought* (London: Oxford University Press, 1934).

Luce (A.A.), "Malebranche et le Trinity College de Dublin", *Revue philosophique de la France et de l'étranger* 128 (1938): 275-309.

Luce (A.A.), *The Life of George Berkeley of Cloyne*, (London: Nelson, 1949).

McCracken (Charles J.), "Stages on a Cartesian road to immaterialism", *Journal of the History of Philosophy* 24 (1986): 19-40.

McCracken (Charles J.), "Berkeley's Cartesian concept of mind: the return through Malebranche and Locke to Descartes", *Monist* 71 (1988): 596-611.

Pucelle (Jean), "Berkeley a-t-il été influencé par Malebranche?", *Études philosophiques* (1971): 19-38.

Vesey (Godfrey), *Reason and Experience: Berkeley* (Milton Keynes: The Open University Press, 1982).

Wild (J.), *George Berkeley, A study of his life and philosophy* (London: Oxford U. P., 1936), esp. 228-243.

> See also *McCracken* and *Lyon* from "General" literature on Malebranche and British philosophy above.

POPE, Alexander (1688-1744)

Hamm (V.M.), "Pope and Malebranche, a note on the Essay on criticism", *Philological Quarterly* 24 (1945): 65-70.

HUME, David (1711-1776)

Bontadini (Gustavo), "Il fenomenismo razionalistico de Cartesio a Malebranche", *Rivista di filosofia neoscolastica* 30 (1938): 249-277.

Brunschvicg (Leon), *L'experience humaine et la causalité physique* (Paris: Alcan, 1922).

Church (R.W.), "Malebranche and Hume", *Revue Internationale de Philosophie* I (1938): 143-161.

Doxsee (C.W.), "Hume's Relation to Malebranche", *Philosophical Review* 25, 5 (1916): 692-710.

Hendel (Charles), *Studies in the Philosophy of David Hume* (Indianapolis: , 1963): 49-57.

Keller (A.), *Das Kausalitäts-Problem bei Malebranche und Hume* (Rastatt: Greiser, 1899).

Laird (John), *Hume's Philosophy of Human Nature* (London: Methuen, 1931).

Novaro (Mario), *Die philosophie des Nikolas Malebranche* (Berlin: Mayer & Muller, 1893).

Pra (Mario dal), "Malebranche nell'opera di Hume", *Rivista di storia della filosofia* 4, 4 (1949): 297-9.

Theau (Jean), "Le critique de la causalité chez Malebranche et chez Hume", *Dialogue* 15 (1976): 549-564.

Verme (Maria Eugenia Dal), "Di alcuni rapporti fra Malebranche e Hume" in ed. A. Gemelli, *Malebranche nel terzo centenario della nascita* (Milano, Vita e pensiero, 1938), 303-311.

Wright (John P.), *The Sceptical Realism of David Hume* (Manchester: Manchester U.P., 1983).

(D) MALEBRANCHE AND EIGHTEENTH CENTURY PHILOSOPHY IN GERMANY

LEIBNIZ   See above under "Malebranche and his contemporaries".

KANT, Immanuel (1724-1804)

Alquié (Ferdinand), "Science et métaphysique chez Malebranche et chez Kant", *Revue philosophique de Louvain* 70 (1972): 5-42, also appendix to the author's *Le Cartésianisme de Malebranche* (Paris: Vrin, 1974).

Ferrari (Jean), *Les sources française de la philosophie de Kant* (Paris: Klinksieck, 1979).

(E) MALEBRANCHE AND ITALIAN PHILOSOPHY THROUGH THE EIGHTEENTH CENTURY

GENERAL

Banfi (Antonio), "Malebranche et l'Italie", *Revue philosophique de la France et de l'étranger* 125 (1938): 253-274.

Includes Fardella, Gerdil and Giovenale.

Berthé de Bésaucèle (Louis), *Les cartésiens d'Italie* (Picard, 1920), Ch. 4.

Includes Giovenale, Trevisan, Zannotti and Gerdil.

Bouillier (Francisque), *Histoire de la philosophie cartésienne* (Paris: Durand, 1854), Vol. II, Chs. XXII-III.

Gives particular attention to Fardella and Gerdil.

Maugain (Gabriel), *Étude sur l'evolution intellectuelle de l'Italie de 1657 à 1750 environ* (Paris, Hachette, 1909).

Werner (Karl), 'Die cartesisch-malebranchesche Philosophie in Italien', *Sitzungberichte K. Akademie der Wissenschaften*, Wien, Klasse 102 no 1-2 (1883): 75-141, 679-754.

Study of Fardella and Gerdil.

VICO, Giam Battista (1668-1744)

Badaloni (Nicola), "L'idée et le fait dans la theorie de Vico", *Les études philosophiques* 24 (1968): 297-310.

Chaix-Ruy (Jean), *La formation de la pensée philosophique de J.B. Vico* (Gap: L. Jean, 1943), 78-81.

Columbu (Mario), "La dottrina delle cause occasionali in Nicola Malebranche e in G. B. Vico", *Sophia* XVIII, 3-4 (1950): 338-347.

Guisso (Lorenzo), *G.B. Vico fra l'immanesimo e l'occasionalismo* (Roma, Perella, 1940).

Lantrua (Antonio), 'Malebranche e il pensiero italiano dal Vico al Rosmini', in ed. A. Gemelli *Malebranche nel terzo centenario della nascita* (Milano, Vite e pensiero, 1938), 337-360.

Scerbo (Giuseppe), *G.B. Vico e il cartesianismo a Napoli* (Roma, Signorelli, 1933).

See also *Banfi* and *Berthé de Bésaucèle* above.

GERDIL, Giacinto Sigismondo (1718-1802)

Ollé-Laprune (L.), *La philosophie de Malebranche* (Paris: Ladrange, 1870), II : 217-232.

See also "General" literature on the reception of Malebranche in Italy above.

(F) MALEBRANCHE AND THE HISTORY OF SCIENCE

Costabel, Pierre, "Le participation de Malebranche au mouvement scientifique", in Centre International de Synthese, *Malebranche, l' homme et l'oevre, 1638-1715* (Paris: Vrin, 1967).

Hankins (Thomas), "The influence of Malebranche on the science of mechanics during the eighteenth century", *Journal of the History of Ideas* 28 (1967): 193-210.

Hobart (Michael E.), *Science and Religion in the Thought of Nicolas Malebranche* (Chapel Hill: University of North Carolina Press, 1982).

Nedelkovitch (D.), "Malebranche et Boskovitch", in Centre International de Synthese, *Malebranche, l' homme et l'oevre, 1638-1715* (Paris: Vrin, 1967).

Robinet (André), "Les Academiciens des Sciences Malebranchistes", *Malebranche Vivant*, OCM XX 162-176.

Robinet (André), *Malebranche, de l' Academie des Sciences. L' oevre scientifique* (1674-1714) (Paris: Vrin, 1970).

For a fuller bibliography of works on Malebranche in the history of science and mathematics, see the Bibliography in *Hobart* above.

III OTHER RECENT MALEBRANCHE BIBLIOGRAPHIES

Robinet (André), "La bibliographie des études malebranchistes", in *Oevres Complètes*, Tome XX, 333-442.

Robinet's bibliography covers the whole of the ninetcenth century and the twentieth century up to 1967.

Sebba (Gregor), *Nicolas Malebranche, 1638-1715, A preliminary bibliography* (Athens: Georgia U.P., 1959).

Although now a little dated this remains a valuable guide to the literature. A revised edition is being incorporated into a special volume of the *Journal of the History of Philosophy* and published by the Southern Illinois University Press, under the title *Bibliographia Malebranchiana 1638-1988*, edited by Thomas M. Lennon, Patricia Easton and Gregor Sebba.

INDEX

Abbadie (Jacques)	136f
abstraction	37
abstractionism	36, 39, 43
Academics	14, 15, 19
active intellect	68
Acworth (Richard)	151, 153, 155
Alquié (Ferdinand)	9, 39, 73, 77, 78, 151
Ameline (Claude)	133
André (Yves Marie)	74, 79, 140, 145, 151
anthropologies	53
Aquinas	36
archetype	25
Aristotelian	35
Aristotle	14, 36, 68
Arnauld (Antoine)	3, 5, 35, 37, 38, 42, 44, 55, 56, 60, 61, 67, 75, 88, 95, 99, 102, 105, 109, 110 133, 134, 135, 147
Astell (Mary)	138
Augustine	7, 49, 67, 68, 72, 79
Augustinianism	64, 66, 79
Averroës	68
Azouvi (François)	153
Banfi (Antonio)	158
Basselin (R.)	138
Bayle (Pierre)	97, 99, 103, 145, 147, 155
Bergmann (Gustav)	25, 47
Berkeley (George)	3, 4, 30, 38, 109, 117, 139, 155
Berthé de Bésaucèle (Louis)	158

bibliographies	159
Bibliothèque Nationale	10
bien général	69, 71
Bossuet (Jacques-Begnine)	6, 9, 53, 59, 132, 145, 148
Bouillier (D.R.)	141
Bouillier (Francisque)	145, 153, 158
Boursier (Abbé Laurent-Francois)	62, 76, 139, 145,
Boussuet (Jacques Benigne)	53, 133, 145, 148
Bracken (Harry M.)	3, 5, 25, 35, 34f, 155
Bréhier (Émile)	73, 153
British philosophy	4, 153
Brown (Stuart)	3, 4, 81, 131, 149
Brunet (Claude)	152
Brunschvicg (Léon)	25, 47, 147, 156
Buffier (Claude, S.J.)	140, 142
Carracioli (L.A.)	141
Cartesian	5, 50, 59, 60, 97, 149, 153
Cartesianism	10, 19, 65, 77, 151
Cartesians	9, 23, 24, 40, 85, 121, 122, 158
causation	116, 121
cause	65, 67, 70, 83, 84, 85, 155, 156
[See also under 'occasional causes']	
Chinese philosophy	149
Chomsky (Noam)	40
Church (R.W.)	116, 156
Collier (Arthur)	6, 8, 154, 156
Condillac (Étienne Bonnot de)	140, 153
Connell (Desmond)	43
consent	69, 80
constant conjunction	125
conventionalism	96

162

Conversations chrétiennes	66, 132, 143
Cook (Monte)	43, 147
Costabel (Pierre)	77, 159
Creation	86
custom	121, 125
Damiron (Jean Philibert)	145
Dawes Hicks (G)	45
De Biran (Maine)	6, 153
De la Forge (Louis)	39, 40
De la recherche de la vérité	50
De la Ville (Louis) nom de plume of L. Le Valois, S.J.	132, 136, 146
de Mairan (J.J. Dortous)	7, 9, 67, 139, 145, 151
Deism	6
Délectation	69, 71
Deprun (Jean)	151
Descartes	5, 23, 26, 32, 37, 38, 39, 42, 43, 59, 67, 78
Desgabets (Robert)	132, 146
desire	98, 101
determinism	71
Deus ex machina	66, 86, 87
Dialogue Between a Christian Philosopher and a Chinese Philosopher on the Existence and Nature of God	144
Dialogues on Metaphysics and Religion	144
direct	36
distance	112, 150, 154
divine intellect	118
divine light	102
divine will	56
divisibility of matter	15
Dortous de Mairan [see under 'de Mairan']	

163

Doxsee (C.W.)	116, 157
Dreyfus (Ginette)	58
Du Terte (Rudolphe)	57, 74, 139, 145, 151
dualism	65
empiricism	4, 102, 154
empiricist	4, 44, 97
England	6
enthusiasm	96, 102, 103
Entretien d'un philosophe chrétien et d'un philosophe chinois	138, 143
Entretiens sur la Métaphysique et sur la Religion	135, 143
epistemological likeness principle	23, 30
epistemology	125
error	95
eternal truths	5, 64
evil	58, 59
Examination of P. Malebranche's Opinion...(Locke)	103, 136
extension	17, 37, 38
external objects	125, 127
external world	115, 139
faith	15
Fall	57
Fardella (A.)	137, 158
Faydit (Pierre-Valentin)	137, 145
Fénelon (François Salignac de la Mothe)	62, 68, 76, 132, 139, 145, 147
fideism	17, 87, 89, 92, 103
Fontenelle (Bernard le Bovier de)	134, 139, 150
form	36
Foucher (Simon)	3, 5, 8, 14, 19, 22, 30, 32, 39, 82, 131, 135, 145
France	6

164

free agents	69
free will	49
French philosophy	151
Gassendi (Pierre)	20
general laws	51, 54, 62, 75
general will(s)	49, 54, 58, 60, 61, 88, 98, 151, 153
Genesis	59
geometry	25
Gerdil (Giacinto Sigismondo)	6, 140, 158
Germany	157
Ginsberg (Morris)	92
Giovenale (Ruffini)	158
God's will	38
good	97, 99, 101
Gouhier (Henri)	25, 34, 78, 146
Grace	78, 82, 96, 138
graces	56
grammar	44
Hardouin (Jean, S.J.)	140, 145
Helvétius (Claude Adrien)	141, 142
Hendel (Charles)	116
Hennert (J.F.)	142
historiography	116
history of science	159
Hobbes	42, 60, 63, 71, 76
Holbach (Paul Heinrich Dietrich, Baron d')	142
Huet (Pierre-Daniel)	3, 5, 7, 10, (Ch. 2 *passim*)
Hume (David)	3, 4, 30, 114, 116, 140, 141, 156
idea	22, 29, 36f., 67, 69, 83, 94f., 111f., 133, 141f., 147ff., 154ff., 158

Idealism   6

immaterialism   115, 155, 156

immortality   89

Index   5, 8

inesse   84

innate ideas   36, 40, 149

inquiétude (anxiety)   98, 100, 101

intellect   119

intellectual intuition   95, 102

Intelligible extension   22, 23, 25, 38, 40

intelligible species   36

intentionality issue   41

intuition   23

Italian philosophy   157

Italy   6

Jansenism   35, 44, 54, 58, 71

Jesuits   5, 10, 57, 58, 145, 151

Johnson (Samuel)   6

Julie de Wolmar   50

Jurieu (Pierre)   54, 74, 133, 135

justice   61, 64, 77

Kant (Immanuel)   49, 60, 157

Kemp Smith (Norman)   28

Keranflech (Charles Hercule de)   6, 141, 142,
                                       143, 153

knowing process   24

knowledge   39, 43, 44

l'Hôpital (Guillaume)   81

Labbas (L.)   145

Laird (John)   44, 116, 157

Lamy (Bernard)   133, 145, 148

Lamy, Francois   45, 136, 137, 145, 150

Lanion   145

Laporte   25

Laws of grace   5

Le Valois   5

[See also under 'De La Ville (Louis)']

Le Vasseur (Michel)   136

Leibniz (G.W.)   3, 4, 34, 52, 56, 57, 64, 72,
                                       81, 96, 119, 133, 134, 138, 139, 145

Lelarge de Lignac (Abbé Joseph-Adrien)   141, 152,
                                                                153

Lelevel (Henri)   136, 145

Lennon (Thomas M.)   41, 43, 129, 154

Lewis (Geneviève)   75

liberty   71, 79, 100

Locke (John)   3, 4, 39, 63, 68, 76, 79, 80, 88,
                                  89, 94, 111, 114, 135, 136, 138, 145, 154

Lovejoy (Arthur D.)   38, 41, 44, 45

Lowde (James)   96, 137

Lyon (Georges Henri Joseph)   154

Malebranche (Nicolas) *passim*

Malebranchisme   6

Malebranchiste   8

Marion (Jean[Luc)   77

Marquer, Louis, S.J.   138, 151

Martin (R.N.D.)   94

Masham (Damaris)   96, 137

material objects   115

materialists   123

mathematics   118

matter   24

Maugain (Gabriel)   158

167

McCracken (Charles)   4, 8, 40, 79, 117, 122, 129, 154, 156

Mechanical philosophy   82

mechanism   79

Meditations (Descartes')   42

Meditations chrestiennes et métaphysiques   133, 143

Meslier (Jean)   142, 152

metaphysics   95

microcosm   84

mind   42

miracles   55, 57, 86, 87, 88, 89, 92, 142

mirror   83

Modern philosophy   86

Molyneux (William)   71, 96, 103

Montcheuil (Yves de, S.J.)   145

Montesquieu (Charles Louis de Secondat, Baron de)   140, 152

moral choice   95

moral psychology   96

moral truths   118

Nadler (Steven M.)   45

Naigeon (Jacques André)   142

natural judgment   13, 116, 118, 125, 126

natural laws   51

natural modalities   81, 88

Nature   50, 81, 84, 85, 89

Nature et grâce   50, 53, 54, 59, 65, 67, 73
[See also under *"Traité de la Nature et de la Grâce"*]

necessary connection   85, 117, 120, 121, 124

necessity   117

Netherlands   100

Newton (Isaac)   26, 124

Newtonians	88
nominalism	99, 103
Norris (John)	6, 96, 135, 136, 138, 153, 154
Norton (David Fate)	7, 153
Oakeshott (Michael)	76, 78
objective presence	110, 111
occasional causes	98, 158
occasionalism	3, 22, 30, 31, 49, 65, 69, 77, 81, 82, 84, 87, 89, 92, 121, 123, 146, 150
occasionalists	85, 86, 114, 117, 120
Ockham	36, 43
Oeuvres Complètes	131, 143
Ollé-Laprune (L.)	145, 152, 159
omnipotence	64
ontology	32
optimism	147, 150
Oratorians	7, 35, 149
outer objects	109, 111
outness	113
Pagan Philosophers	85
Pantheism	85
particular wills	49-54, 60, 75
Pascal (Blaire)	20, 54, 60
Paul (St.)	64
perception	65, 111
perfection(s)	50, 56, 63, 69, 82
Pillon (François)	145
Plato	64
Platonism	25, 68, 72, 77, 82
pleasure	97, 100
Pope, (Alexander)	156

Popkin, (Richard H.)   3, 5, 10, 20, 33

Port Royal Logic   35, 42

Positivists   31

Postigliola (Alberto)   75, 153

pre-established harmony   81, 87

predestination   96, 100

Prémotion physique   80

presence   110

presentational realism   43

Prévost (A.F.)   140, 152

Providence   54, 55, 57, 62, 138

Pyrrhonism   18, 19, 68

qualities   22

Quesnay, (François)   152

Quietisme   147

Radner (Daisy)   45

Randall (John Herman Jr)   25, 33

Rationalism   12

Realism   36, 154

Reason   119, 128, 135

Recherche de la vérité   5, 10, 25, 59, 67, 69, 76, 82, 116, 131, 143, 146

Réflexions sur la prémotion physique   62, 64, 70, 80, 139, 143

Régis (Pierre-Sylvain)   60, 75, 135, 150

Reid (Thomas)   38, 111, 117, 142

Remond (Nicolas)   81

representationalism   45, 147, 148, 154

representative ideas   35, 36, 41, 43, 44

representative theory of perception   111, 112, 154

resemblance   24

Riley (Patrick)   4, 5, 9, 49, 145, 151, 153

Robinet (André)   77, 131, 143, 147, 149, 150,
                                      151, 152, 153, 159

Roche (A.M.)   141

Rousseau (Jean-Jacques)   50, 60, 141, 152

royalists   35

sceptical fideism   12

scepticism   14, 19, 22, 87, 127

Scholastics   17, 35, 84, 99

Schrecker (Paul)   25, 34, 47

Scotus   36

Scripture   53, 54, 55, 59

Search after Truth   3, 109, 110, 113, 126, 136,
                                                           144

Sebba (Gregor)   8, 131, 159

secondary causes   65, 86, 87, 96

Seeing all things in God   16, 38, 43, 67, 68, 83,
                                      95, 114, 115, 136, 138

self   116, 137, 155

sensations   25

sensible extension   27

sentiment   111

Sergeant (John)   137

Sextus Empiricus   39

siècle des lumières   7

sin   56, 96, 103

soi-même   136

spatial presence   110

Spinoza   9, 14, 71, 151

Spinozism   6

stereoacuity   113

Stolius (G.)   140

171

Suarez   43, 46

substance   37, 84

substance philosophy   31

substance/property ontology   22

sufficient reason   119

suspense   101, 102, 103

Taylor (Thomas)   6, 136, 138, 154

Théodicée   64

theodicy   55, 58, 150

Thomas   16

Thomistic   36

Tiedemann (D.)   143

Tractatus Theologico-Politicus   14

Traité de la Nature et de la Grâce   5, 9, 35, 45, 49, 50, 52, 97, 132, 143, 145

Traité de morale   52, 66, 118, 143

transubstantiation   5

Treatise of Nature and Grace   85, 95, 136, 144

Trevisano (Bernardo)   138, 158

truths of mathematics   119

understanding   98, 102, 103

uneasiness   101

union of the soul and the body   86

utilitarian analysis of Malebranche   98

vérités éternelles   77

Vesey (Godfrey)   3, 4, 109, 156

Vico (Giambattista)   138, 140, 158

Vienne (Jean Michel_   3, 4, 94

vision in God [See under 'Seeing all things in God']

volition   67, 80, 98

volontés générales [See under 'general wills']

volontés particulières [See under 'particular wills']

Voltaire (François-Marie Arouet de)   64, 141, 145, 152

voluntarism   49, 72

Watson (Richard A.)   3, 5, 22, 33, 91, 146

wax example   23, 38

Werner (Karl)   158

Wheatstone (Charles)   113

will   3, 49, 57, 71, 72, 80, 97, 98, 101, 103, 104, 118, 119

willing   70

wisdom   51, 55, 56, 58, 61, 62

Wittgenstein   30, 31, 32

Wright (John P.)   3, 4, 116, 157

Yolton (John W.)   35, 38, 39, 43, 46, 111, 154

Zannotti (Francesco Maria)   158

HOBBES STUDIES

Editor-in-Chief:

Martin A. Bertman
3146, Terrace Drive
Riverside, Cal. 92507
U.S.A.

Publisher:

Van Gorcum & Comp. B.V.
P.O. Box 43
9400 AA Assen
the Netherlands
Tel.: 05920-46846
Fax: 05920-72064

Subscription:

Hfl. 50.00 (individuals)
Hfl. 65.00 (libr. & inst.)
Hfl. 40.00 (members IHA)

Publication:

annualy

Initiated at the 400th anniversary of Thomas Hobbes' birth, (1988) this journal hopes to be a focus for Hobbes scholarship, in conjuction with the *HOBBES NEWSLETTER* and the International Hobbes Association.

The journal intends to publish papers on every aspect of the work and life of Thomas Hobbes. But, further, in considering Hobbes to have left a still useful and alive intellectual legacy, this journal encourages engagement and criticism of his thought....for the sake of a clearer and more responsible understanding of man and the world.

Thus, the journal is committed to both scholarship and debate, with Hobbes as its focus; and it encourages historians of ideas, legal theorists, literary critics, political scientists, philosophers and psychologists to mention those fields where Hobbes has a conspicuous following, to contribute to it.